fragrant GARDENING

fragrant GARDENING

Steve & Val Bradley

with photography by Andrea Jones

MURDOCH
BOOKS

CONTENTS

1
The search for scent

2
Designing a fragrant garden

3
The fragrant garden in spring

CONTENTS

4
The fragrant garden in summer

5
The fragrant garden in autumn

6
The fragrant garden in winter

introduction

Scent is the oxidisation of essential oils found in the flowers and leaves of plants, but it is far more important than a simple chemical process. The fragrance of a flower or the aroma of a leaf lifts the spirits and gladdens the heart. From roses and honeysuckle growing around a secluded seat in high summer to wintersweet and winter jasmine flowering near a doorway during the coldest months, there are plants that can perfume your garden throughout the seasons.

Types of scent

Scented plants give life to the garden and make simply being there a pleasant experience. However, just as plants vary greatly in terms of colour and size of bloom, they also differ in fragrance. The scent of some plants is bold and intense, while the scent of others is more delicate and subtle – the choice is at the discretion of the gardener. For example, if you prefer floral fragrances, you could choose the intoxicating aroma of hyacinths (*Hyacinthus*) or the sweet scent of lily-of-the-valley (*Convallaria majalis*). However, if you prefer fresh, herby scents, you could choose the pine-like aroma of rosemary (*Rosmarinus officinalis*) or the stimulating fragrance of chives (*Allium schoenoprasum*).

Outdoor living

These days, outdoor living is taking increasing precedence, partly because houses are becoming smaller and the weather warmer. Where gardens were once considered ornamental or productive, now we expect much more from them. They are still for sitting and relaxing in, but also for playing, entertaining and dining in, and there is no reason why even a small garden cannot accommodate these aspects as well as a host of delightful

fragrances. In a large garden, you may choose to place a scented plant so that it becomes a focal point and draws attention by its sheer presence. In a small area or on a patio, you can grow the plant in a container and move it to wherever it will be closest to you, in order to appreciate its beauty. This might be near a door that you use frequently, under a regularly opened window or adjacent to the dining area so that you can enjoy the fragrance while entertaining friends.

Attracting wildlife

Fragrant plants attract insects to the garden, and if you want to create a wildlife-friendly garden you can even use a specific scent to encourage a particular species. Bees and butterflies prefer sweet scents such as lavender (*Lavandula*); moths are attracted to flowers that are fragrant during the evening such as night-scented stock (*Matthiola bicornis*); beetles like the fruity scents of plants such as lemon balm (*Melissa officinalis*); and flies prefer foetid smells such as stinking Benjamin (*Trillium erectum*). Birds are attracted by colour rather than fragrance, but you can combine the two by planting crimson and gold varieties of scented flowers such as *Primula* and *Crocus*.

Uses of scent

Scent is not just an attractive feature for the garden. Scented plants can also be used in the home in a variety of ways, and the flowers and leaves do not even have to be fresh to be of benefit. The essential oils of many fragrant plants are used in aromatherapy, because their healing properties are recognised as aids to the body and spirit. Dried flowers can be used in potpourri, lavender bags and sleep pillows to aid relaxation, scent the atmosphere and keep moths away from clothes in a cupboard. The dry bark of *Eucalyptus* gives potpourri a refreshing aroma, and the leaves of herbs can be dried and stored for use in cooking and medicinal preparations even when the plants themselves are dormant. Bunches of herbs hung in the kitchen can repel flies in summer, and leaves thrown on the barbecue while you cook can deter biting insects.

Planning your garden

The aim of this book is to show you how, with a little planning and preparation, your garden can be a source of fragrance throughout the year. The first chapter examines the history of

Plants such as this Asclepias *will fill your garden with summer fragrance as well as attract pollinating insects.*

scented plants and explains how scents are classified. It then looks at the many ways in which essential oils can be used as well as how to harvest and dry the different parts of plants. The second chapter guides you through the basic principles of garden design, enabling you to make the most of fragrance no matter what size of area you are dealing with.

This garden design has used a mixed planting scheme to create a pretty pond area surrounded by fragrant and colourful flowers.

Season by season

The remainder of the book is divided into four chapters, one for each season of the year. Each chapter contains information about fragrant plants for the season in question and explains the jobs you may need to do in the garden at that time of year. There is also advice on the selection, cultivation and propagation of a wide range of plants. In addition, each seasonal chapter features several projects, with clear photographic steps, to help you achieve some wonderful effects with fragrance in your

garden. These range from basic techniques such as propagating a fragrant plant to more elaborate undertakings such as creating a scented walkway.

Plant directories

At the end of each seasonal chapter you will find a plant directory that describes some of the fragrant plants that flourish at that time of year, from trees and shrubs to perennials and annuals, and with scents ranging from fruit to honey and cloves to violets. For each plant there is a photograph, a description of its physical characteristics and fragrance, plus advice on pruning and propagation.

chapter one

1

A fragrant history

The use of scent dates back to the earliest civilisations and has played a role in food preservation, medicine and human ritual ever since. Spices and gums such as cinnamon and frankincense have been popular preservatives for millennia. In the sun-baked, arid area known today as the Middle East – one of the main centres of early civilisation – trees were highly valued. Their leaves provided much-needed shade for people and animals, and the volatile oils given off in the heat were so refreshing that branches were cut and placed indoors. The use of perfumed oils dates back to the ancient Egyptians, who distilled parts of flowers and plants for application to their bodies both in life and death. The word perfume itself derives from the Latin *per*, meaning 'through', and *fumum*, meaning 'smoke', denoting its early value as incense.

The Garden of Eden

Written 4,000 years before the birth of Christ, the Bible's Book of Genesis describes how the Garden of Eden was created by God as an earthly paradise. Research has shown that the garden was located between the Tigris and Euphrates rivers, in an area known as Babylonia. The river that irrigated the garden flowed on to the land of Havilah, where gold, onyx and bdellium were found. Bdellium is possibly the prickly shrub *Commiphera myrrha*, from which the aromatic resinous gum myrrh is obtained. In the days before alcohol was developed as a means of dissolving the essential oils of flowers, myrrh was much prized for its strong and long-lasting fragrance.

The spice trade

Trading in spices and aromatics – the scented leaves and bark of plants, dried or distilled – began about 2000BC with the Egyptians, and caravan routes quickly developed around Egypt, Arabia and Palestine. The most commonly traded substances were myrrh, spices and a balm that was extracted from trees and used for burning as incense, chewing or, later, for flavouring drinks by the Greeks. Jericho was a major trading point for local goods such as cedar wood, believed by the Egyptians to last forever. It was much sought after for use in coffins and as cedarwood oil, one of the most expensive body oils. Aromatic spikenard (*Nardostachys jatamansi*) was brought from the Himalayas, and Arabia yielded the fragrant gum frankincense, prized second only to myrrh.

As civilisation spread, more plants were discovered and trade expanded. Egypt traded copper and turquoise for sandalwood trees (*Santalum album*) and various incense trees. Plant products such as saffron, aloe, cinnamon and ginger became desirable commodities and flowers were also highly prized, including lilies (*Lilium*), lotus (*Nelumbo*) and water lilies (*Nymphaea*). Roots were perhaps the most valuable part of a plant because they could be dried and stored. One of the oldest recorded plants, *Iris florentina*, has strongly violet-scented roots and the intensity increases as the roots wither, until they eventually smell more like violets than violets themselves. Ground into the powder known as orrisroot, they were used whenever fragrance was desired.

Evening primrose (Oenothera biennis) has long been prized for its medicinal benefts as well as its sweet fragrance. The oil obtained from its seeds is considered to be particularly therapeutic.

Many scented plants were also spread from country to country by invaders. The Romans, for example, introduced ginger (*Zingiber officinale*) to the colder climates of northern Europe, growing it on a hot-bed system over composting material. They were also responsible for spreading many herbs, including chives (*Allium schoenoprasum*), rosemary (*Rosmarinus*), sage (*Salvia officinalis*) and thyme (*Thymus*), from their warm Mediterranean habitats to the northerly outposts of the Roman Empire.

Early use of fragrance

The Greeks used fragrant oils to ward off illness, sprinkled furnishings with scented waters and placed garlands of fragrant flowers around the necks of their guests. They also used perfumes and flowers in funeral rites. The Greek philosopher and scientist Theophrastus (*c.*370–*c.*287BC) wrote an early study of perfumes entitled *Concerning Odours*. He described how a poultice on the leg could sweeten the breath by the essences permeating the skin and entering the circulatory system.

The Romans adopted many Greek uses for perfumes. Saffron crocus (*Crocus sativus*) was highly prized and used in cooking, as a dye and in oils. Saffron is the dried stigma of the autumn crocus, which ripens only in hot, dry weather. It has more commercial uses than almost any other plant, but is expensive, as 70,000 blooms are needed to produce just 500g (1lb) of saffron. The Romans liked to prove their wealth by strewing saffron on the floors of their villas.

Roses (*Rosa*), hyacinths (*Hyacinthus*), myrtle (*Myrtus*) and jonquil (*Narcissus jonquilla*) were popular in 7th-century Eastern civilisations, where the wealthy surrounded themselves with plants that were aromatic or produced strongly fragrant flowers. Musk was the most popular fragrance, and the followers of Mohammed mixed it with mortar when building their places of worship, to give lasting fragrance. The Koran mentions that the floor of the Garden of Paradise is covered with wheaten flour mixed with musk and saffron. Musk-scented roses grew throughout Syria, and their use is traditional as oils and unguents, and as petals either strewn or floating in bowls of water.

Many Hindu ceremonies use fragrant woods, flowers and perfumes. In India, roses (*Rosa*) and jasmine (*Jasminum*) are used to make perfumed oil. Traditional Indian medicine, *Ayur veda*, uses essential oils and dates back to 1000BC. In China, jasmine flowers are used to make fragrant tea. Fragrant flowers are also hung in the house and temple on festive occasions.

Scent in medieval times

In medieval Europe, flowers were used to decorate churches on festive days. They were cultivated in monastery gardens along with the herbs used for medicinal and culinary purposes. The packed-earth floors and small windows of the times also meant that buildings and churches smelled musty, so fragrant seasonal flowers, herbs and sweet-smelling grasses and rushes were strewn on the pews and floors. The scented rush *Acorus calamus* had numerous uses in addition to strewing: it also yielded a volatile oil from the leaves, and the root could be used to flavour beer and wine, or could be dried and powdered for use as talcum powder. Herbs were particularly useful for strewing because they released a fragrance when walked upon. For many years, royal households had an official 'Strewer of Herbs'.

Other plants were used for their repellent abilities rather than fragrance. Green rushes strewn on floors could attract fleas and other insects, so it was customary to burn repellents such as fleabane (*Erigeron acris*) to avoid infestation. Rue (*Ruta graveolens*) was used in the sickroom to drive away disease-carrying bugs.

From Renaissance to present day

Pomanders were another popular ward against disease, and Elizabethan pomanders consisted of a dried orange or lemon stuck with cloves, or a container with a sponge soaked in scented vinegar. Later, silver pomanders were made, based on the orange, with filigree segments hinged at the base and held by a clasp at the top, each of which could hold a separate perfume.

In the 16th century, sprinkling scented water on furnishings and fabrics became fashionable throughout Europe. Flowers and leaves were distilled in the large houses of the wealthy for personal use, cooking and as medicine. The kitchen garden would provide rose petals and numerous herbs that could be used fresh or dried. Clothes and linens were stored in chests made from fragrant wood, such as sandalwood, cedar or juniper, so that the scent would permeate the fabric.

Cloves, orris powder, lemon and oils of thyme and spikenard could be used to make perfumed waters or a dry potpourri to fragrance a room. Itinerant salesmen would sell cheap substitutes such as roseroot (*Sedum rhodiola*, now *Rhodiola rosea*), which grew freely on walls and cliffs and smelled of rose when the root was crushed, and beads of hardened gum moulded using hands dipped in jasmine oil so that the scent was absorbed.

Both the Greeks and Romans had used powdered root as talcum powder, and it was also widely used in Elizabethan times. The powder might be inserted in a sachet and used to fragrance linen, dusted onto a lady's hair or blended as snuff. Linen sachets would contain orrisroot or the powdered roots of herbs. Many dried leaves were powdered and used in snuff, which was taken to clear the head of a cold and improve the temperament. At the time of Shakespeare, combinations of orrisroot and chamomile (*Chamaemelum nobile*) were popular.

Perfumes also came into general use during this time, when exotic new fragrances were brought back from the New World and other far-flung locations. Queen Elizabeth I, for example, was given a pair of scented Italian gloves, probably fragranced with frangipani. Similar to jasmine, frangipani is distilled from the flowers of *Plumeria*, a sweet-smelling flower found in Antigua, Jamaica and Martinique.

Contemporary fragrance

Scented flowers and aromatic gardening fell into decline during the 18th century when landscape gardening, with its emphasis on dramatic vistas rather than floral displays, began to come to prominence. The Victorians remedied this to some extent with their love of flower beds, although they tended to concentrate on colour rather than fragrance. By the turn of the 20th century, however, the aromatic garden had begun to rise again in popularity and, in more recent times, there has been a strong revival of interest in both aromatherapy – the use of aromatic plant extracts and essential oils for healing and cosmetic purposes – and gardening. Fuelled to a large extent by the need to relax from the stresses of modern life, the garden is seen as the perfect haven, filled with a healing blend of fragrant plants.

Commercially, the interest in aromatic plants has never been more intense. Perfume is a huge industry, and many Hollywood celebrities vie with one another to name a best-selling fragrance. The town of Grasse in southern France is one of the largest centres in the world for the production and development of fragrances, and devotes much financial investment to intensive plant-breeding programmes designed to produce varieties with greater concentrations of sought-after essential oils.

Dried leaves, flowers, berries, spices, peel and bark were used to make potpourri in the 16th century. Often enhanced with essential oils, the mixture helped to fragrance the home and mask unwanted smells.

Classification of scent

Scent appeals to the olfactory senses just as music appeals to the ear. There is a range of odours in the same way that there is a scale of notes, and a perfume needs to have its notes in harmony or there will be discord. Certain odours blend naturally together, such as almond, vanilla and heliotrope, or patchouli, cedar and sandalwood. On a higher 'octave' come verbena and citron, and even higher comes the combination of rose, petit-grain and neroli (orange blossom, derived from the Seville orange, *Citrus aurantium*). Combinations such as these occur throughout the plant kingdom, and it is said that the perfumer has 4,000 raw materials to work with – the finished perfume can be likened to the creation of a symphony.

Reactions to scent

The sense of smell is the most basic of human senses. Scents are detected by tiny filaments at the top of the nose, where olfactory cells connect directly into the central nervous system. Too much perfume overpowers these sensitive nerve endings and reduces the ability to appreciate the scent. Different people also respond in different ways to scent, with dark-haired people having a keener sense of smell than fair-haired ones, making perfumes notoriously difficult to categorise.

Some scents are best enjoyed from a distance because they change when they are too concentrated. For example, the aroma of *Rosa foetida* is pleasant from afar, but too close and the smell becomes that of rotten fish due to the presence of indole (a natural plant chemical that is also present in rotting animal tissue). Indole is also responsible for the cloying sweetness of flowers such as lily (*Lilium*) and jonquil (*Narcissus jonquilla*). Another plant chemical, aminoides, is found in white or off-white flowers and can make them smell of ammonia and attract flies.

The fragrances of some plants, such as *Narcissus* and hyacinths (*Hyacinthus*), tire the olfactory nerves so that, from being initially attractive, the scent becomes less pleasant and, in the case of violets, changes to the smell of cut cucumber or damp moss. The fragrance of leaves is seldom as oppressive as that of flowers due to the presence of different chemicals, such as geraniol, which is found in the rose-leaf geranium (*Pelargonium capitatum*).

The reaction to scent is not purely a question of aesthetics. Perfumes also have a definite effect on health. Violets (*Viola*), for example, have rendered singers unable to produce a note by affecting their vocal chords. Beans and night-scented stock (*Matthiola bicornis*) have an effect like intoxication, and the common gorse (*Ulex europaeus*) is reputed to cure headaches with its fresh, fruity scent.

Constituents of scent

Fragrance is not composed of a single substance but is actually a composite of chemicals exuded by different parts of the plant. The most pure – and difficult to imitate – is the essential oil generally found on the upper side of the petals or sepals of the

The flowers of the Citrus limon *are classified in the Lemon group of scents. They have the same tangy fragrance as the fruit.*

flowers. As the plant develops, the cells of the flower (which at first contain only chlorophyll) change to hold other substances, such as tannin or the essential oil. The oil is stored with sugars as a 'glycoside' in cells from which the protoplasm (original cell contents) has been removed. The fragrance is released as the glycoside decays, a process that slows or stops at certain times of day or if the flower closes again. Some oils are more volatile than others, with those having a low degree of volatility (such as patchouli and cedar) being classed as stronger than those with a high degree (such as lavender).

Flower perfume groups

Although the scents of flowers are wide-ranging, there are several clearly identified perfume groups. However, since some flowers fall between groups and identification tends to be personal, these cannot be exactly quantified.

- **Heavy group**
  Strong, lasting scents and flowers that are often white or cream in colour, such as *Lilium candidum*, *Philadelphus*, lilac (*Syringa*) and lily-of-the-valley (*Convallaria majalis*).

- **Aromatic group**
  Pleasant fragrances of cinnamon, clove, vanilla and balsam, including pinks and carnations (*Dianthus*), *Viburnum carlesii*, hyacinths (*Hyachinthus*) and night-scented stock (*Matthiola bicornus*).

- **Violet group**
  A sweet scent that can tire the senses, such as *Iris reticulata*, *Acacia* and mignonette (*Reseda odorata*).

- **Rose group**
  A light, sweetly fruity fragrance, including rose-leaf geranium (*Pelargonium capitatum*).

- **Lemon group**
  A refreshing, tangy fragrance, such as *Rosa bracteata*, *Oenothera odorata* and *Nymphaea odorata*.

- **Fruit-scented group**
  A wide-ranging group (all fruit scents except those in the Lemon group), including *Philadelphus* (orange scent), *Cytisus battandieri* (pineapple), *Freesia* (ripe plums), *Rosa wichuraiana* (green apples), *Rosa soulieana* (ripe bananas) and *Iris graminea* (apricots).

- **Animal-scented group**
  Scented of cats, dogs, foxes, goats or human sweat, such as *Fritillaria imperialis*, *Hypericum*, ox-eye daisy (*Leucanthemum vulgare*) and *Codonopsis*. Musk-scented flowers include *Rosa moschata* and *Muscari muscarimi*.

- **Honey-scented group**
  Closely related to musk-scented flowers, with a delicate, sweet fragrance, including *Buddleja*, *Sedum spectabile* and honeysuckle (*Lonicera*).

Leaf perfume groups

Leaf scent is more subtle than that of flowers. However, while a flower's perfume reduces when dried, leaf fragrance is persistent and can increase as the water evaporates, concentrating the essential oils. Some of the same oils are found in both leaves and flowers. As a result, some leaf fragrances conform to flower-scent groupings, including many *Pelargonium*, which fall into the Rose or Lemon groups. Apple mint (*Mentha suaveolens*) and *Rosa rubiginosa* (formerly *R. eglanteria*) smell of apples and fall into the Fruit-scented group, as does *Salvia sclarea*, a hardy biennial with leaves smelling of fresh grapefruit when bruised. Leaves also contain some different oils from flowers, such as pine scent.

- **Turpentine group**
  A resinous aroma, such as rosemary (*Rosmarinus*).

- **Camphor and Eucalyptus group**
  A medicinal scent that clears the nasal passages, including sage (*Salvia officinalis*), chamomile (*Chamaemelum nobile*), *Eucalyptus*, thyme (*Thymus*) and myrtle (*Myrtus*).

- **Mint group**
  A tangy, fresh scent, such as *Mentha* and *Pelargonium*.

- **Sulphur group**
  A heavy, cloying smell, including onions (*Allium cepa*) and garlic (*Allium sativum*).

Stems and bark

Freshly cut timber has a soft, warm fragrance, and many woody plants have fragrant stems, gum and/or bark. Bog myrtle (*Myrica gale*) has wood and leaves with a sweet, lemony fragrance when crushed. *Hebe cupressoides* has stems and leaves with a light bouquet of violets, and sweet gum (*Liquidambar styraciflua*) has a balsamic scent. Plants with scented bark fall into two categories.

- **Aromatic group**
  Includes cinnamon (*Canella winteriana*), *Eucalyptus*, *Betula lenta* (a warm, spicy scent like wintergreen) and *Illicium anisatum* (incense-scented).

- **Turpentine group**
  A resinous aroma, including conifers such as fir (*Abies*), Scots pine (*Pinus sylvestris*) and larch (*Larix*).

Roots

Several plants have fragrant roots, although the scent is not detectable unless the plants are dug up. Blessed herb (*Geum urbanum*) is a herbaceous perennial with short, thick, rhizomatous roots that smell of cloves when dried. Chocolate root (*Geum rivale*) is moisture loving with thick, rhizomatous roots smelling of chocolate. Other plants with fragrant roots include liquorice (*Glycyrrhiza glabra*) and sweet flag (*Acorus calamus*), which produces a camphor-like smell and was used in the past as a strewing herb for floors. *Iris pallida* and *I.* 'Florentina' both have roots that smell strongly of violets when dried and powdered.

Fungi

Various fungi have distinctive smells, not all of them pleasant, although they tend to change as the fungus matures. Some, such as the stinkhorn (*Phallus impudicus*), attract flies to spread their spores by smelling of rotting flesh or fish. Others smell of damp woodland, garlic, sulphur, goat or musk. The more pleasant scents include cloves, anise, violet, rose and fruit.

Seeds

Many plants have seeds that can give rich scents and flavours to food and drink, usually by crushing. Aniseed (*Pimpinella anisum*) gives a liquorice flavour to cough mixtures, liqueurs, soups, sweets and cakes. Caraway seeds (*Carum carvi*) flavour bread, cakes, cheese, soups and liqueurs. Coriander seeds (*Coriandrum sativum*) have an orange-like fragrance when dry. They are used in pickles and curries and, with sugar, in the making of sweets. The seeds of dill (*Anethum graveolens*) have a spicy bouquet and are added to cakes, bread, fish and rice dishes. Fennel (*Foeniculum vulgare*) has the flavour of liquorice and complements oily fish such as mackerel.

The leaves of the garlic plant (Allium sativum) *are classified in the Sulphur group, with a heavy, cloying scent.*

How plants use scent

Everything in nature evolves for a reason and the fragrance in plants is no exception. Scent performs two main functions: it attracts pollinating insects and protects the plant from pests. But why do some plants have a strong fragrance while others have none at all? And why are there so many different fragrances? These questions can be answered by looking at the life cycle of the plants themselves and the environment they inhabit – for example, bees are attracted to the colour blue, so some plants that grow in areas colonised by bees produce blue flowers and therefore have no need of scent. Natural evolution is not the only factor determining a plant's fragrance, however. Over the years horticulturists have bred many plants to enhance or reduce certain characteristics, including scent.

Protection

Plants can use the essential oils in their leaves and stems to deter attack by pests and browsing animals. The oils almost become a replacement for thorns. For example, ants seem to dislike the scent of mint intensely and will avoid it at all costs, so the dwarf creeping form of the plant (*Mentha pulegium*) can be useful to have around the entrances to the home to deter these insects from entering.

Many highly aromatic plants originate in hot, arid areas where they protect themselves from desiccation by releasing oils that remain in a vapour immediately around the surface of the leaf. The effect is further enhanced if the leaf is covered with hairs that can trap the vapour.

Pollination

All plants rely on pollination to ensure the continuation of the species. Different plants have different methods of ensuring that pollination takes place. Some, like birch (*Betula*), oak (*Quercus*) and conifers, use wind dispersal of pollen; others, such as *Elodea*, use water. The majority, however, rely on insects. This allows cross-pollination between plants, so that genetic material is constantly mixed and the resultant plants are strong and healthy.

Scent is an important way of attracting pollinating insects. It is more noticeable on a calm, warm day, especially in a sheltered spot or under trees, since the more sheltered the location, the more the plant relies on fragrance to attract insects because they are less likely to be brought past on the wind. Plants that grow in shaded places or flower during the night are especially fragrant. Most night-flowering blooms open for a single night and die after fertilisation. The lower temperatures and higher humidity levels of evening and night-time trigger the release of fragrance. Many flowers that open at night, such as Italian honeysuckle (*Lonicera caprifolium*), are pale colours such as white, cream or pale yellow, with long, tubular flower parts.

Many different insects can be involved in the pollination process, and each is attracted by a different means. Competition to attract them is fierce and some plants have very specific relationships with the pollinating agent. A mutual dependence can evolve so that the life cycles of both insect and plant are closely connected.

Bees are attracted by certain colours and markings, so flowers such as this Rosa 'Complicata' *do not need to have a strong scent to attract them.*

Butterflies and moths

Both belong to the Lepidoptera group and have long, tubular mouth parts for penetrating deep into the flower. Butterflies visit flowers such as the honeysuckle (*Lonicera periclymenum*) in the day and early evening, while moths pollinate night-flowering plants. Flowers that rely on butterflies and moths are usually strongly scented because these insects are attracted by perfume. Butterflies are especially attracted to shrubs such as lavender (*Lavandula*), privet (*Ligustrum*), lilac (*Syringa*) and *Buddleja*, and herbaceous perennials such as *Aster*.

Bees

Bees belong to the insect class Hymenoptera, have well-developed eyesight and are primarily attracted by certain colours (particularly blue) and markings that direct the insect towards the centre of the flower. They appear to be red/green colour-blind and show little interest in flowers of these colours. Blue flowers often have very little scent since the colour is sufficient to attract the pollinating agent.

Flies

Not all insects enjoy pleasant scents. Flies of the insect class Diptera, for example, delight in disgusting smells with no appeal to other insects. Plants that attract flies include yellow skunk cabbage (*Lysichiton americanus*), stinking Benjamin (*Trillium erectum*), lords-and-ladies (*Arum maculatum*), stinking hellebore (*Helleborus foetidus*) and fetid bugbane (*Cimicifuga foetida*).

Birds

Many birds appear to be blue/green colour-blind and, where they are responsible for flower pollination, the predominant flower colours are crimson and gold. The colour attracts the pollinators, with fragrance having no part to play.

Beetles

The few flowers that rely on pollination by beetles usually emit a fruity scent to attract them. They are also fully open because beetles have short tongues and could not otherwise reach into a tubular-shaped bloom.

Colour and scent

Colour and scent do not go hand-in-hand; fragrance is often a substitute for colour, and the brighter the colour, the less scent there is. Since both are a means of attracting pollinating insects, one element of the plant's make-up is compensating for another. The heaviest fragrance occurs in white flowers and those with thick, waxy or velvety petals. Thinner petals cannot retain essential oils, so fragrance is quickly lost. The more pigment or chlorophyll present in the petal, the less oil is produced, so those with an absence of coloration, such as lily-of-the-valley (*Convallaria majallis*), white carnation (*Dianthus*) and pheasant-eye narcissus (*Narcissus* 'Actaea'), contain the most oil.

The strength of fragrance in relation to flower colour can be simplified, from strongest to weakest, as: white, cream, pale yellow, yellow, pale pink, mauve and purple. Flowers that are orange, red, blue or brown tend to have little or no fragrance because they contain so much pigment. The Clematis family, with a colour range from white to deep purple, is a good example of the interrelationship of colour and fragrance. The winter-flowering *Clematis rehderiana* (pale creamy yellow) smells like cowslips; the spring-flowering *C. armandii* (pure white) is strongly scented; and the summer-flowering *C.* 'Duchess of Edinburgh' (white) is one of the few large-flowered hybrids to have any scent. The darker forms seldom have any scent at all.

The less pigment a flower contains, the stronger its scent. White flowers such as this Clematis armandii *have the most powerful fragrances.*

Family characteristics

Plants are categorised into families by the arrangement of their floral parts, but the scent given off by members of the same family can be quite similar. For example, all the members of *Papilionaceae* (the Pea family), including sweet pea (*Lathyrus odoratus*), broom (*Cytisus/Genista*) and gorse (*Ulex*), have a lemon-vanilla fragrance. Some plant families have little or no scent, such as *Scrophulariaceae* (including *Nemesia*, *Penstemon*, *Phygelius* and *Antirrhinum*). Scent cannot be bred naturally into these plants because the ability to produce it has not developed in their make-up. They rely entirely on brightly coloured flowers to attract pollinating insects.

Hybridising plants

The 19th-century Austrian botanist Gregor Mendel was the first person to analyse the characteristics passed from one generation of plants to the next. He used the pollen from one plant to fertilise another, giving a limited range of possible options in the next generation. Plants inherited features from each parent, but also characteristics from previous generations that were not obvious in either parent. He concluded that hidden characteristics, though present in each generation, could be masked by a stronger element of the same feature.

Hybridising is the crossing of two plants to obtain a given result. In those cases where this can be virtually guaranteed to produce a similar result every time, the offspring is known as the F1 (or first-cross) generation. F1 plants have 'hybrid vigour', which means they produce plants that are bigger, with larger flowers or more fragrance. F2 plants are produced by crossing two F1 hybrids and the results are less uniform.

Breeding for scent

Pollen from a chosen variety has to be carefully applied, in isolation, to a selected mother plant and the resultant seed harvested and sown. Out of a batch of seedlings, just one or two might be chosen from thousands because they have more fragrance. It can take several generations to achieve a desired result. Sometimes, the selection of one characteristic will outweigh others and, over a period of years, one aspect of the plant will decline. For instance, when colour is bred into flowers, the scent is often lost. This happened in roses, where breeding concentrated on flower colour and size, and resistance to diseases like rust. An increased desire for fragrance has led some breeders to cross-refer back through a plant's lineage to ascertain where the scent gene weakened. They can then breed back to a rose that still had a strong scent. Ideally, the fragrance can be reintroduced without losing the benefits of the modern flower.

Breeding plants for scent is a painstaking process since just one or two seedlings from a batch of thousands could have the required fragrance.

Essential oils

Essential oils are the concentrated natural chemicals within the plant that contain fragrance. Although they are often used simply as perfume, they also have therapeutic value. When applied by massage or in baths, the oils penetrate the skin and quickly enter the bloodstream and lymphatic system. The inhalation of the aroma is also believed to affect emotions and mood. A belief in the healing powers of essential oils dates back to the earliest times. Primitive humans, for example, used antiseptic gum from trees such as conifers, balsam poplar (*Populus balsamifera*), walnut (*Juglans*) and birch (*Betula*) to ease sore throats and treat cuts. Nowadays, oils such as cinnamon, clove, verbena, geranium, lavender and rosemary are widely used to treat a range of health problems, from headaches and colds to insomnia and anxiety.

Types of oils

Essential oils may be held within various parts of the plant, including the flower, leaf, bark, roots and rind. Oils extracted from fragrant leaves have a greater antiseptic strength than those obtained from petals, with the exception of attar of roses, which is a strong antiseptic. The oil is stored in the leaf in several ways. It may be held deep within the leaf or in capsules that require pressure to release the oil; in cells on or near the surface, to be released when the temperature rises; or in glandular hairs on the underside of the leaf. In flowers, the oil is stored in cells from which the chlorophyll has been withdrawn, on both surfaces of the petals, although the concentration is usually greater on the upper surface. There is a wide range of alcohol and other chemicals involved in creating each individual scent derived from the essential oils of flowers.

Obtaining essential oils

Removing the essential oils from the plant without losing the fragrance is at the heart of perfume production. Commercially, this may be done by several methods, including extraction, distillation, expression and enfleurage. If you wish to make your own essential oils rather than buy them, you can do so using a simplified home enfleurage process.

Extraction

The oil is gently washed from the flowers using a chemical solution to obtain the most concentrated essence. The solvent produces a thick, concentrated wax that is identical in perfume to that of the original flower.

Distillation

Flowers able to withstand heat and produce a large amount of scent for their weight, such as rose and orange blossom petals, are placed in a large tank and steam is driven through them. The oil can then be separated from the water since the two substances do not mix.

Expression

The raw material – usually citrus rind – is compressed in order to release the oil. Water is then used to separate the waste material from the oil.

The fresh flowers of Lavandula angustifolia *are used to make lavender essential oil. Lavender oil, with its sweet floral scent, is renowned for its ability to relax the body and uplift the mind.*

Enfleurage

Sometimes known as absorption, this expensive method is suitable for delicate flowers that will not withstand chemical or heat treatments, such as lily-of-the-valley (*Convallaria majalis*), violet (*Viola*) and jasmine (*Jasminum*). These flowers continue to give off oils after harvesting, so they are laid on glass sheets and covered with vegetable oil that gradually absorbs the fragrance. The flowers are changed daily for up to a month so that the vegetable oil contains as much fragrance as possible. Alternatively, the flowers may be spread onto muslin sheets soaked in olive oil. After a month, the cloth is squeezed to remove the olive oil saturated with scent. The vegetable oil or olive oil is then treated to separate the scent from it.

Home enfleurage

To produce small quantities of your own essential oil, gather the dry flowers of the plant you wish to use, remove the stalks and place the flowers in a glass jar half-filled with good-quality olive oil. After 24 hours, remove the flowers, squeeze them (allowing the liquid to run back into the jar) and then discard the flowers. Add some fresh flowers to the jar. Repeat this process until the oil is saturated with perfume. Finally, add an equal quantity of pure (ethyl) alcohol, screw a tight lid onto the jar and shake daily for two weeks. The fragrant alcohol can then be poured off the olive oil and used.

Buying and storing oils

Although it can be satisfying to produce your own oil, buying essential oils is the quickest and easiest option since there are many different oils available from a wide range of producers. Always read the label before you buy to see where the company sources its ingredients and if it runs checks for purity. If the oil is labelled as 'aromatherapy oil', it will probably have been mixed with a carrier oil such as grapeseed oil. Although this is necessary if you wish to apply essential oil to the skin through massage, for example, it does reduce the oil's life from years to months.

All essential oils oxidise over time, so look for oils sold in dark-tinted glass bottles and avoid any that have been on display in a hot window, since heat and sunlight accelerate the deterioration process. Try to keep the bottles firmly sealed as much as possible and store them in a cool place such as a refrigerator. When blending your own oils, use a glass eye dropper (available from your local pharmacy) to measure the quantities of oil and always shake the bottle well before use. Remember to label the bottle, too, and include the date of purchase.

Using essential oils at home

There are many ways in which essential oils can be used around the home to have a beneficial influence on both you and your surroundings. Depending on which fragrance is selected, the effect can be relaxing or stimulating, and can even be enhanced if oils are used in combination.

Baths

After a busy day in the garden, add 5–10 drops of your favourite essential oil to a filled bath and then lie back and enjoy. The water should not be too hot or the fragrance will be lost quickly. Having an aromatherapy bath is also ideal for relieving stress, especially with a relaxing oil such as lavender. Other oils you might like to try include bergamot and jasmine for depression; neroli and ylang ylang for anxiety; eucalyptus and peppermint for headaches; and chamomile and juniper for aches and pains.

Massage

Essential oils are highly concentrated and should be diluted in a carrier oil, such as grapeseed or jojoba, for skin application. This also helps the hands to glide smoothly. The scent of the carrier oil should not overpower the essential oil – olive oil, for example, aids itchy skin but tends to be strongly scented. For every 50ml (2oz) of carrier oil, add 20 drops of essential oil for use on the body; 10 drops for use on the face; and 5–10 drops for use on children. Each essential oil has its own properties and can be matched to the occasion. Try clary sage and basil for tiredness; peppermint and ginger for nausea and digestive problems; sweet marjoram and rose for insomnia; and patchouli and sandalwood to increase sex drive.

Vaporisation

Ceramic burners usually consist of a shallow saucer over a night-light candle. The heat from the candle causes drops of oil (either used alone or in a small quantity of water) to evaporate and scent the air. Alternatively, place a few drops of oil in a dish of water on a radiator or in a sunny window. Eucalyptus has a refreshing scent; bergamot is stimulating; basil increases concentration; rose improves the mood; and lavender is relaxing. In the car, place a few drops of an oil such as peppermint on a small sponge or tissue to help you stay alert during a journey.

Potpourri

Refresh the scent of fading potpourri by adding a few drops of your favourite essential oil. Rose, citrus and spice oils are ideal for this, either alone or in combination.

Perfume

Essential oils need to be mixed with alcohol in a ratio of about 1:5 oil to alcohol in order to preserve their scent as perfume. Alternatively, a few drops of oil on a tissue tucked discreetly into your clothing will last for several hours. By mixing oils together, you can create a unique fragrance to suit your own personality and preferences. Using oils in this way can also be therapeutic. If you are having trouble sleeping, for example, a few drops of lavender, basil, chamomile or clary sage oil on your pillow or a tissue nearby should help you relax and enjoy a good night's sleep.

Steam inhalation

Many essential oils have active antibacterial and antiseptic properties, and can be used as a steam inhalant. For a cold, try adding 5–8 drops of eucalyptus oil to a large bowl of hot water. Lean over the bowl, place a towel over your head and breathe in the vapour for about 10 minutes. Repeat two or three times a day. *Warning:* Anyone suffering from asthma should not use steam inhalation.

Compresses

Therapeutic oils such as chamomile, lavender, rosemary, juniper, birch and ginger can also be applied to the body using hot and cold compresses. Use hot compresses to relieve muscular aches and pains, and cold compresses to soothe headaches and tension. Add 5–10 drops of oil to the hot or cold water and stir well. Soak a cloth or towel in the water, then squeeze out the excess and place the cloth on the affected area. Leave in place until the compress begins to cool down or heat up, then repeat for up to an hour.

Warning

Do no apply undiluted essential oils to the skin and avoid citrus oils prior to exposure to the sun. If you have sensitive skin, test first with a small amount of oil to check for a reaction. Never massage areas of the body with broken skin, rashes, swollen joints or varicose veins. Anyone with a heart condition should avoid massage. Expectant mothers and people with high blood pressure or epilepsy should consult a qualified aromatherapist before using essential oils.

The flowering tops of Rosmarinus officinalis *produce essential oil with a pine fragrance. The antiseptic qualities of rosemary oil make it effective against skin irritations and a useful ingredient in hair tonics.*

Harvesting & drying

The flowers, leaves, seeds, roots and bark of plants can be harvested, dried and stored for future use. It is important to harvest different parts of the plant at different times of the year and to dry them correctly. This will ensure that the harvested plants are in the best condition, retaining as much of their fragrance, flavour and other properties as possible. Once you have mastered this process, there are numerous books available containing recipes and remedies that use plant produce as ingredients. One of the easiest and most popular ways in which to use plant material is potpourri. This is usually a fragrant mixture of garden produce in an ornamental bowl, and may be dry or moist (a combination of pickled flowers and leaves).

Leaves

For the best results, it is important to harvest leaves when they are at their peak. This means that they should be mature but not beginning to show signs of ageing. To make sure you get the best flavour or fragrance – from plants such as lemon verbena (*Aloysia triphylla*), *Pelargonium*, bergamot (*Monarda didyma*), rosemary (*Rosmarinus officinalis*) and sage (*Salvia officinalis*), for example – aim to harvest in mid-summer before the plant flowers, although the exact timing will be dictated by the weather conditions. After flowering starts, the chemical balance within the plant changes and the oils in the leaves are not as potent. Pick them in the morning after the dew has dried and the plant has begun to warm up, but before the day becomes too hot, discarding any damaged leaves and those close to flowers.

With most plants, it is easier to cut whole stems because they can be handled without damaging the individual leaves. Bundle them together in bunches of 5–10 stems, depending on their thickness, and secure them with an elastic band (as the stems dry out and shrink, they often fall through the loop if they are tied with string). Hang the bunches upside down in a dark, warm, well-ventilated place such as an airing cupboard until they are dry. Drying time will depend on the thickness of the stems involved and can vary from days to weeks. For cooking, herb leaves should be crumbled between finger and thumb and stored in dark, airtight glass jars with labels until they are needed. For potpourri, the leaves can be left whole.

Flowers

Like leaves, flowers should also be harvested when they are at their peak. It is best to do this in the middle of a dry day, when the flowers are fully open but not beginning to fade. Remove the whole flower with some of the stalk to avoid damaging the petals, then check them carefully and discard any damaged ones. Place the flowers in an open container so that they do not begin to sweat, which can lead to rotting.

Dry large flowers by hanging them in bunches in a dark, warm, well-ventilated area in the same way as leaves. Lay small flowers that are difficult to hang, such as borage (*Borago officinalis*) or violets (*Viola*), on sheets of muslin stretched over a wooden

Always harvest flowers when they are at the peak of their condition and before they begin to fade. Remove them by the stalk to avoid causing any damage to the delicate petals.

frame or metal cooling rack. Dried correctly, flowers should retain almost all of their colour. Once dry, the petals or whole flowers are ready to use – in potpourri, for instance. If storing them for future use, flowers such as lavender (*Lavandula angustifolia*) and chamomile (*Chamaemelum nobile*) can be stored intact; others, like marigold (*Calendula officinalis*), need to have their petals removed.

Seeds

Seeds such as juniper berries, vanilla pods, dill seeds, nutmeg and cloves should be fully ripe before harvesting, with no visible sign of green remaining. Collect them on a warm, dry day by shaking the seed head into a paper bag or cutting whole seed heads and laying them on paper in a seed tray. Put them in a dark, warm, well-ventilated location and allow to dry. Many seeds will turn brown or black when they dry, but not all, so test them for firmness to check whether they are dry or not rather than rely on their colour. Store dried seeds in packets or envelopes in a dark, airtight jar until they are needed.

Bark

The bark of some trees, such as *Eucalyptus*, cedar (*Cedrus*) and sandalwood (*Santalum album*), peels readily and can be collected, preferably from younger stems. Do not pull at the bark or you may damage the tree, and never remove a circle of bark right around the trunk or the tree will die. Dry pieces of bark by laying them on a muslin-covered frame in a warm, dark location in the same way as flowers.

Roots

Both roots and rhizomes from plants such as angelica (*Angelica archangelica*), ginger (*Zingiber officinale*), sweet iris (*Iris* 'Florentina'), sweet violet (*Viola odorata*) and valerian (*Valeriana officinalis*) should be harvested in autumn, when the foliage is dying down and the concentration of oils is at its strongest. Remove the required amount and replant the rest of the plant so that it will survive for the next season. Wash the soil from the roots, handling them very carefully to avoid damaging or bruising them. Lay the roots on baking trays and dry them in an oven, turning them regularly until they break easily, then cool and store in an airtight glass or metal container.

Drying temperature

As soon as a flower or leaf is detached from the plant, changes begin to take place within the cells because their supply of moisture is cut off. The quicker the piece of plant material can be dried, the quicker this process is frozen, trapping the oils within the cells. However, the process must be controlled because drying too quickly, in an oven for example, allows the remaining moisture to evaporate too quickly, taking the oils with it. If dried too slowly, however, the oils are destroyed by decomposition. Ideally, flowers, leaves, seeds and bark should be dried in a dark, warm, well-ventilated location, such as an airing cupboard or warm loft, aiming for a temperature of around 20°C (80°F). The exception is roots, which can be dried in the oven at about 50°C (120°F) because they need higher temperatures to dry properly.

Dry potpourri

Dry potpourri mixtures are easiest to make using dried leaves, flowers, berries, spices, peel or bark, along with a fixative to preserve the blend. Fixatives are available as powders and often have their own fragrance that must be taken into account when choosing the mixture of ingredients. The most common fixative is orrisroot, with its violet scent, and is used in a ratio of about 15ml (1tbsp) of orrisroot to every 250ml (1 cup) of plant material. Essential oils are ideal for refreshing old potpourri, but add only a few drops at a time or the fragrance will be overpowering.

The choice of plant material suitable for making potpourri is wide-ranging, so it is always possible to create a fragrance to suit your personal tastes. You can also tailor scents to different areas of the home – for example, you could opt for a warm, spicy mixture in a hallway or a sweet, floral bouquet in a bedroom. You could also design your potpourri to reflect the changing seasons (see seasonal plant directories for ideas). Listed here are just a few of the plants you might like to choose.

- **Scented flowers**
  Honeysuckle (*Lonicera*), hyacinth (*Hyacinthus*), jasmine (*Jasminum*), lavender (*Lavandula*), lilac (*Syringa*), mock orange (*Philadelphus*), rose (*Rosa*) and violet (*Viola*).

- **Aromatic leaves**
  Basil (*Ocimum basilicum*), bay (*Laurus nobilis*), bergamot (*Monarda didyma*), lemon balm (*Melissa officinalis*), mint (*Mentha*), rosemary (*Rosmarinus*), sage (*Salvia*), sweet cicely (*Myrrhis odorata*) and thyme (*Thymus*).

- **Fragrant spices, peels and roots**
  Allspice, cinnamon, clove, ginger, juniper, nutmeg and star anise; all types of citrus peel; roots of cowslip (*Primula veris*), sweet flag (*Acorus calamus*) and valerian (*Valeriana*).

Herb and lavender dry potpourri

250ml (1 cup) lavender flowers (Lavandula angustifolia)
125ml (½ cup) dried spearmint (Mentha spicata)
125ml (½ cup) marjoram (Origanum majorana)
125ml (½ cup) oregano flowers (Origanum vulgare)
30ml (2tbsp) powdered orrisroot
10ml (2tsp) lavender essential oil

Mix the ingredients together well, then place in a plastic bag for two weeks to mature, shaking regularly. Display in an ornamental bowl.

Moist potpourri

This traditional method uses the highly fragrant petals of the damask rose (*Rosa damascena*) or cabbage rose (*Rosa centifolia*) as the main ingredient and produces a potpourri that will last for several years. Part-dry the rose petals until they are leathery and halved in bulk (about two days in good weather), then layer them with sea salt in a ratio of 250ml (1 cup) of salt to 750ml (3 cups) of petals. Alternate layers in a bowl until it is two-thirds full, then stand it in a dark, dry, well-ventilated place for 10 days until the ingredients are caked together. Break the 'cake' into pieces and mix with any other fragrant ingredients in the recipe in an airtight container. Let the mixture ferment for six weeks, stirring daily. Add any dried flowers and essential oils for the final two weeks.

Rose and spice moist potpourri

1 litre (4 cups) fermented rose petals (see above)
90ml (6tbsp) powdered orrisroot
30ml (2tbsp) ground mace
30ml (2tbsp) ground allspice
15ml (1tbsp) ground cloves
1 nutmeg, grated
1 cinnamon stick, loosely crushed
15ml (1tbsp) crushed bay leaves (Laurus nobilis)
15ml (1tbsp) citrus peel
250ml (1 cup) dried rosebuds

Following the instructions outlined above, ferment all the ingredients together except the dried rosebuds for four weeks, then add the rosebuds and ferment for another two weeks. Transfer the potpourri to a decorative container. Cover the container when not in use to preserve the potpourri's fragrance.

Roses (Rosa) are a traditional ingredient in potpourri. The dried petals can be used in dry potpourri or they can be fermented and used as the basis of a moist potpourri that will last several years.

chapter two

2

Assessing your garden

Whether you are giving an old garden a new look or starting from scratch with bare ground, you will need to ascertain a few basic points to help you choose the right plants for the right locations. Remember that a garden is a long-term investment in both time and money, so it makes sense to do a little research before you begin. It will pay dividends over the years, with your plants thriving rather than struggling or, worse, having to be replaced. You also need to assess the garden in terms of existing features and factors such as privacy and size, and adjust your design accordingly – a well-placed hedge can increase the privacy of your garden and reduce the amount of noise entering it as well as introduce fragrance, for instance.

Orientation and location

The orientation of a garden is the direction it faces – that is, the direction from which it receives the most direct sunlight. You can use a compass to be exact, or simply watch the progress of the sun throughout the day, noting which areas are the hottest and which get no sun at all. You have no choice over the orientation, but it will influence the plants you can use in these areas, since shade-lovers will scorch in the sun and sun-lovers will become drawn and sickly in the shade.

Another factor to take into account is the location of your garden. Do you live in an urban area where temperatures are usually warmer and the situation more sheltered; an exposed rural setting where the temperature is cooler and frost more common; or a coastal area affected by salt-laden winds but less severe temperatures? All of these factors will affect which plants will do well in your particular garden.

Soil type

Knowing what type of soil you have will also help you determine the plants that best suit your garden. To identify the type of soil, rub some between your fingers. If it does not stick together, you probably have sandy or silty soil; if it feels gritty but does stick together, it is most likely to be a loam soil; if it sticks together readily with a shiny surface, it is clay soil. Loam soils are ideal for most plants; sandy and silty soils drain freely and are therefore suitable for plants that can cope with dry conditions; clay soils drain slowly and are perfect for moisture-loving plants.

pH level

As soil forms, it is influenced by local factors such as the underlying rock type and these have an effect on the soil's acidity or alkalinity. The exact nature of your soil can be measured on what is known as the pH scale – a scale from 1 to 14, with 1 being the most acidic and 14 the most alkaline – using a small soil-testing kit available from garden centres. Every plant has a pH range in which it will thrive, and another in which it can survive. A pH of 6.5 to 7 is regarded as neutral, or suitable for a wide range of plants. Below this, the soil will be too acidic for lime-loving plants (calcicoles) such as *Dianthus*. Above pH 7, it will be too alkaline for acid-loving plants (calcifuges) such as

If you know the pH level of your soil, you can choose plants that will thrive in those conditions. This Rhododendron cubittii *prefers acidic soil with a pH level of less than 6.5.*

Rhododendron. If your soil has extreme pH levels, the only way to grow plants from the opposite group is to keep them in containers, where you have complete control over the growing conditions. Knowing the pH level of your soil can save you from making costly mistakes like buying a plant that is unsuitable for the conditions and unlikely to survive.

To test your soil, take five small samples (free from stones and plant debris) from a depth of about 10cm (4in) at different points around the garden. Mix them together in a plastic bag. Following the manufacturer's instructions provided with the soil-testing kit, test a small amount of soil from the bag. Once the test is complete, the colour of the clear liquid in the sample can be compared against the chart supplied with the kit to show the overall pH level of your garden. Alternatively, a single test sample will show the pH in a specific part of the garden.

Existing features

Unless you are designing a new garden for a bare patch of ground, you will probably have to work around existing features. Some of these, such as a greenhouse on a brick base, will be fixed, but others might be movable, even if they have to remain on site. Wooden sheds, for example, may be moved to another location, provided a stable new base can be created. When drawing a plan of the garden (see page 44), remember to indicate features such as these straight away so that you do not overlook them later when you are creating your design. There are some existing features, such as oil tanks, compost containers and dustbins, that are best hidden from view, and planning a new design is the ideal time to hide or disguise them. Tall plants, climbers, trellis or woven screens are all methods of making what could be an unsightly area into an attractive one.

Privacy

Many people regard the garden as an extension of the living area – a room outdoors. As such, the need for privacy while entertaining or relaxing is more important than ever. At the same time, new houses and gardens are getting smaller and more closely packed, making privacy in the garden increasingly difficult to attain. Careful planning is therefore vital if you are going to create a garden that is both pleasing to the eye and comfortable to use.

It is natural to want to position your seating area in a sunny spot, so before you begin your design, sit there and assess how exposed it will be and how much that matters to you.

Consider the possible solutions and try to visualise them in place. For example, a neighbouring bedroom window can be screened with an upright plant, perhaps a small tree or upright conifer. More general exposure might warrant a hedge that can be allowed to grow just high enough to screen you without causing disputes with your neighbours over loss of light. Alternatively, you could place a screen immediately around the seating area itself, giving privacy while you are there but keeping the rest of the garden open. If these features are incorporated at the planning stage, there will be no need for a potentially expensive redesign afterwards when you realise there is a problem.

Boundaries

Most gardens have some form of boundary to mark the extent of the property, and larger gardens may have inner boundaries to divide the garden into discreet sections. The type of boundary used – such as walls, fences or hedges – can have a dramatic impact on how the garden looks and feels. In terms of fragrance, a hedge around the perimeter of the garden or around an area within it is ideal. Hedges are less costly than walls, although not as long lasting. The big bonus of using a hedge, however, is that many fragrant plants can be grown as hedges, either as a single variety (see pages 144–145) or mixed as a tapestry hedge.

Tapestry hedges mean that you can combine plants that have different seasons of interest, although their growth rates need to be fairly well matched or one may swamp another. Once the plants are established, you can extend the interest still further by growing climbers through the hedge, to flower when the rest of the hedge is not in season. Choose small- or medium-sized varieties that will not overwhelm the hedge, and avoid twiners such as honeysuckle (*Lonicera*), which can strangle other plants.

Prickly fragrant plants such as *Rosa rugosa* and *Mahonia aquifolium* are ideal for growing as a low boundary hedge to deter unwanted visitors or to prevent people from cutting across the garden. Both have attractive, very fragrant blooms followed by colourful fruit later in the year, giving two seasons of interest. *Mahonia* is also evergreen.

Even if you have existing walls or fences that you wish to keep, you can choose to grow a hedge alongside them in order to introduce fragrance. A simpler solution is to grow aromatic climbers along the boundary, using decorative trellis to train the plants if necessary. If the boundary in question is an open fence, this will also provide some additional privacy.

Pathways

Spend some time moving around the garden and working out the routes you are most likely to use. Mark on your plan of the garden any existing pathways that you wish to keep, and bear them in mind when drawing up your planting scheme so that the pathways become fragrant journeys through your garden. You can also create additional pathways and even change the existing ones altogether if they are not suitable to your needs and tastes. If you do not like an existing pathway but do not want to go to the expense and effort of changing it, you will need to think of ways to incorporate it into your garden design so that it becomes an unobtrusive and even desirable feature. For example, installing an archway covered with overhanging aromatic plants can draw the eye upwards and minimise an unattractive pathway below.

Small gardens

Many houses have only small gardens, particularly newly built ones. However, there are several tricks you can employ in your garden design to make a small area seem larger than it is. You can use increasingly shorter plants as you go farther away from the house, for example. This deceives the viewer into thinking that all the plants in the garden are the same height and that those at the end of the garden are farther away than they really are. Similarly, you can use large-flowered varieties nearby and small-flowered ones at a distance. Another good trick is to keep bright colours close by and use paler ones farther away, so that they appear to blur into the distance and make the end of the garden indistinct.

You can also use shaped trellis on walls to give an increased sense of perspective. Start near the house with trellis that covers the wall from top to bottom, then decrease its size as you move farther away. The mind expects the trellis to be the same size along its length, so the smaller trellis in the distance looks as if it is even farther away than it actually is. Another simple *trompe l'oeil* illusion is to use mirrors. These can be partly hidden behind the planting to give the impression that the viewer is catching a glimpse of another part of the garden through a small window. Align the mirror so that the viewer does not immediately see his or her own reflection or the trick will be spoiled.

A large, solid hedge divides this garden into areas with distinctly different characters. The foreground is filled with a lively profusion of flowers, while the stone pagoda hints at a more tranquil area in the distance.

Choosing a style

Although you need to bear in mind the factors discussed in Assessing Your Garden (see pages 34–37), the style of planting you choose will, to a large extent, be a matter of personal taste. You should start by deciding what you want from your plants. Are you aiming for fragrance throughout the garden, or would you prefer to incorporate scented plants among unscented ones? Do you want all the fragrance to come from flowers, or are you including aromatic foliage? Do you want colour, interest and fragrance throughout the year, or only in certain seasons? Also take into account whether you want to use any of the plants outside of the garden. For example, do you want herbs for cooking or cut flowers to display within the home? Time spent on this part of the planning process will reap rich rewards in the years to come.

Timing fragrance

Depending on when and how much you are likely to use your garden, it may not be necessary to plan for fragrance throughout the year. If, for instance, you rarely venture outside during the winter, then you can devote more attention to plants that are at their best during the other seasons. Alternatively, if fragrance is particularly important to you at a certain time of year, you can concentrate specifically on that season. People who suffer during the dark days of winter, for example, may find it beneficial to pick sprigs of fragrant plants to bring indoors at this time. When we think of fragrance, we usually think of flowers. But plants with fragrant fruits are also a good way of extending seasonal fragrance and interest in the garden when the main flowering season may have finished. Use the plant directories at the end of the seasonal chapters to help you plan scent according to your needs. It is also worth thinking about the time of day that you use your garden. Growing some night-scented plants, particularly near the house, walkways or patios, is a good way of enjoying fragrance and your garden during the evening.

- **Plants with fragrant fruits**
  Drimys winteri, Gaultheria shallon, Helianthus annuus, Illicium majus, Laurus nobilis, Monodora myristica, Podocarpus andinus, Sassafras officinale, Syzygium aromaticum, Zanthoxylum americanum.

- **Night-scented fragrant plants**
  Gladiolus tristis, Hesperis fragrans, Lonicera caprifolium, Mirabilis jalapa, Oenothera triloba, Petunia integrifolia, Silene noctiflora, Sisyrinchium odoratissimum, Verbena teucrioides, Zaluzianskya villosa.

Herb gardens

The use of herbs, both in cooking and in medicine, dates back to the earliest civilisations, and herbs are now undergoing a revival, with an ever-increasing range available. Many herbs originate in the Mediterranean region and therefore grow best in an open, sunny site with well-draining soil. Most herbs need very little space, so you can grow a wide variety in a small area of the garden or you can grow them in containers. Traditional herb gardens are designed so that they can be accessed easily throughout the year, with pathways of brick or gravel to allow

Lonicera and rosemary, intermingled with unscented plants, are used to bring fragrance to a rustic seat in a cottage-style garden.

Allium and Nepeta provide colourful and fragrant ground cover along this pathway, enticing visitors to explore farther into the garden.

the plants to be picked. These may be laid in a pattern based on circles, squares, diamonds or diagonals. Many herb gardens are therefore planted according to a formal structure like a traditional knot garden. However, if you would prefer a less structured look, you could plant the herbs more randomly and use a mixture of pathways and stepping stones to access them.

- **Herbs suitable for growing in containers**
  Allium schoenoprasum, Crocus sativus, Laurus nobilis, Mentha x piperata f. citrata, Mentha spicata var.crispa, Monarda didyma, Myrtus communis, Ocimum basilicum, Tanacetum parthenium, Thymus x citriodorus.

- **Herbs suitable for making a lawn**
  Chamaemelum nobile, Chamaemelum nobile 'Treneague', Mentha arvensis, Mentha pulegium, Mentha requienii, Thymus praecox, Thymus pseudolanuginosus, Vinca minor.

Cutting gardens

The keen flower arranger needs a ready supply of fresh flowers and foliage to cut throughout the year so that the house is constantly supplied with natural fragrance. Annual and perennial plants are ideal for this, but some shrubs are more tolerant than others of this kind of attention. Access to all the plants is important, and stepping stones within the beds are an easy solution. An important thing to note is that this is a labour-intensive style of gardening since plants that are constantly being required to replace cut growth need regular and intensive feeding or their reserves will become depleted and the plant may die.

Annual gardens

Many fragrant annual plants can be dried for use in potpourri and dried flower arrangements. Since annual plants grow, flower and die within a single season, it is possible to condition the soil regularly when the bed is empty. There should be little problem with seedlings from a previous batch of plants appearing the following year since the flowers and seed heads should be harvested for drying before the seed is shed (see pages 28–31).

Mixed plantings

By far the most popular type of garden is one that encompasses a wide range of plants: deciduous and evergreen; flowering and foliage; woody (trees and shrubs) and non-woody (bulbs, annuals and perennials). By having such a wide range, there can be something of interest throughout the year. In general, a garden such as this is designed with smaller plants at the front of borders and beds, and larger ones at the rear. However, it is important to remember that in winter it is not always easy to step onto the soil and, in order to appreciate the fragrance of a plant at this time, it may need to be situated near a pathway or door. Make full use of winter-flowering shrubs that are not interesting during the summer by planting a small- or medium-sized climber to scramble through them. The climber will be dormant in winter when the shrub flowers but come into bloom itself during the summer months. It is possible to combine the beauty of both fragrance and water in the garden. Scented plants can be used to surround a water feature such as a fountain, pond or pool – this is particularly effective if the feature is sited near seating where both can be enjoyed. Alternatively, fragrant water-dwelling plants can be grown in the water to become an intrinsic part of the feature.

Use fragrant plants to bring scent to mixed borders. Here, roses provide a backdrop to a summer border that includes Allium, Salvia *and* Paeonia.

Basic design principles

Beautiful gardens can look as if they were made by the hand of nature alone, with plants growing alongside each other in perfect balance and harmony. This is sometimes the case, but more often such gardens are the result of careful design. Although anyone can produce a garden design, not all designs are destined to be successful when the garden is actually created. Whether you opt for a formal, geometric design or a more rambling, natural look, there are certain basic principles that should be observed if you are to achieve a garden that fulfils all your needs. Questions of balance, harmony, rhythm and scale all need to be addressed. Similarly, it is important to think of the garden as a three-dimensional space, taking into account the height of each feature and plant as well as the length, width and density.

Balance

Each element within the garden occupies space, both physically and visually. Balance is the art of making sure that one area of the garden does not outweigh another. Aim to have each busy area of planting balanced by a corresponding area of calm open ground. This may be a lawn or some gravel, paving or decking. Each area of bright colour needs a complementary area of muted colour, both to make it stand out and to rest the eye when you look away. Without this, the garden could feel crowded, overwhelming and even claustrophobic. There will be no opportunity to stand back and admire the beauty of the planting, and its effect may be lost.

Harmony and rhythm

In music, harmony and rhythm give life to the work, a sense that all the elements flow together as part of the whole, and there is no discord. In the garden, they serve the same purpose, but visually. To achieve a harmonious garden, it is best to follow a common theme throughout the design, rather than add in lots of disparate elements. For example, if you start off with curves, keep curves; do not use straight lines. Likewise, if you start with a rigid geometric pattern, do not be tempted to introduce a curve. It is easier to create a successful, flowing design with blocks of planting rather than individual plants because there is more visual space between the centres of colour. You can then use individual plants as specimens to highlight and accentuate the surrounding block.

A lawn serves the same purpose in the garden that a carpet does indoors – it flows through the different elements of the garden and links them together, just as carpet flows from one room to another to unify an interior decoration scheme. Paving performs the same function. Always try to make your linking feature – whether it is lawn or paving – flow through the design. If you dot it here and there, you will break up the rhythm of the scheme and the whole effect will become disjointed.

Scale

Keeping each feature within the garden in scale with the others, and with the size of the garden itself, will ensure that no single element becomes too dominant. A large tree or pergola will be out of scale in a small garden, and will take up so much space

This rose garden uses a circular design to create a rhythmic flow around the beds of flowers and has a statue in the centre to create a focal point. The arches are positioned symmetrically to keep the design balanced.

that something else will have to be sacrificed. In a large garden, a tiny pergola will be swamped by the features surrounding it and its effect ruined. In a small garden, you can use smaller varieties of plants to scale everything down and give the impression of more room. In a long, thin garden, it is a good idea to use smaller plants farther away to make the garden seem even longer; conversely, putting taller plants at the far end of the garden will make it appear visually closer.

The third dimension

When designing your garden, it is important not to think in just two dimensions; use the third dimension, height, as well. Height can be found in all sorts of places. Walls, fences and trellis can be used around the edge of the garden or introduced in the centre. Obelisks, wigwams and pillars can be inserted in borders, and hanging containers can be attached to posts and filled with trailing plants that will reach down to the plant layer below.

You can use taller plants, or structures with plants covering them, to divide the garden into sections so that the whole garden is not visible at once and the viewer is tempted to walk into it to see what is around the corner. You may not have the space to divide the garden into entirely separate rooms, but you can create compartments even in relatively small gardens.

Focal points

A statue, water feature or special plant can be used as a means of drawing the eye of the observer into the garden and to a desired area. This is useful if there is another, more unsightly feature that you wish to deflect attention away from. If the garden is small, select a scaled-down statue or feature to maintain the element of perspective. Blocks of planting, rather than single plants, can have the same effect, especially if the flowers or foliage are brightly coloured.

Planting opportunities

The biggest problem the keen gardener tends to face is a lack of space – there is always one more plant to be squeezed in somewhere. This is where your imagination can come to the fore. If there is an area of paving, leave gaps between the bricks or stones and plant low-growing subjects into them that can tolerate being stepped on occasionally. Thyme (*Thymus*) is an excellent plant for such situations because it releases a delicious scent when it is bruised and is remarkably resilient. Planting pockets in walls can be filled with trailing thymes, which will thrive in the good drainage.

Wherever you have an established shrub or climber that is dull during part of the year, look for a plant you can grow up through it to flower during the required season. For instance, *Pyracantha* flowers in spring and has brightly coloured berries in winter, but is not particularly interesting at other times of the year. By planting a summer- or autumn-flowering *Clematis* to grow through its branches, you can have colourful flowers in summer, and the *Pyracantha* will support the *Clematis* as it grows. When pairing two plants in this way, you need to make sure that they are well matched or the climber may swamp the host. Honeysuckle (*Lonicera*), for instance, is a strong-growing climber that will strangle all but the most vigorous host. The smaller-growing varieties of climber are ideal.

Basic plan drawing

Once you have assessed your garden, chosen your planting style and considered the basic principles of garden design (see previous sections of this chapter and above), you need to draw a plan of your garden. There is no need to view this as a difficult task, because with a piece of paper, pencil and something to measure with, it is actually very easy. Doing it, however, will give you the opportunity to see how your ideas look when they are marked out, and will provide a point of reference afterwards if you lose any plant labels.

Working from fixed points, such as the corners of the house, measure the distance to various points around the garden. Use at least two measurements for each element of the garden, taken from different places, so that you can pinpoint these elements exactly when you transfer them onto paper. You can use a long tape measure for this or simply stride it out – but make sure only one person does the striding because no two peoples' strides will be the same length. It is easiest to draw the plan on squared paper, using an appropriate scale – one square on the paper equal to 1m (3ft) or one stride, for example.

Once you are happy that you have been reasonably accurate, mark the edges of the house and garden in pencil on a large piece of paper. Add any existing features of the garden that are not going to be moved (a greenhouse on a brick base, for example). It is also a good idea to draw a pointer on the plan to show where north is because this will help jog your memory about sunny borders when you come to finalise your choice of plants. Once you are satisfied with your drawn plan of the existing garden, go over the lines in ink. You are now ready to begin designing your new garden.

Sketch out your ideas on the plan in pencil. You may wish to photocopy the ink drawing of the plan several times in case you need to start again or wish to compare several design plans (always save an unmarked master copy for this reason). When you are satisfied, move outside and begin laying out the design on the ground with whatever materials you have available. For example, you could use a garden hose for pathways, canes for fencing, strings and pegs for borders and beds, and balloons or boxes for shrubs. Doing this will help you see how your design might look in situ – your neighbours may think you have gone a little crazy, but this is the time to find out whether what you have in mind will work.

Stand back, assess the garden carefully and make any necessary adjustments. For example, you may find you have over- or underestimated the size of a feature. It is much easier to decide now than halfway through construction, especially if you are ordering materials such as concrete, paving slabs or topsoil, all of which are difficult to deal with if you order too much.

Detailed planting schemes

When you have finished the basic design plan, you need to draw up detailed planting schemes for each area of the garden. So, for example, if you have indicated on the basic plan that you are going to have a flowerbed near the house, you then need to plan exactly which flowers you are going to use and where they will be sited in relation to each other. This will help you ensure that the chosen plants have sufficient room to grow, taller plants will not hide smaller ones from view and so on. (See pages 46–49 for specific ideas on fragrant planting.)

Maintenance requirements

Before you put your plan into action, spend some time assessing how much maintenance your new garden will need. The following chapters outline the various jobs that may need to be carried out each season. Read them carefully and consider how much or how little maintenance your particular design will involve. Be realistic about the amount of maintenance work you are willing to do – there is no point in going ahead with a wonderful garden design simply to watch it fall into neglect in the years to come.

The plants growing alongside this pathway will need regular pruning to keep them in check. Always consider how much maintenance a garden design will require before beginning to plant.

Making the most of fragrance

There are many different benefits to be gained from growing aromatic plants and, since scent is open to such personal interpretation, each person may appreciate different ones. For most of us, the main benefit of entering a fragrant garden on a mild day is the feeling of rejuvenation that it engenders, an uplifting of the spirit that makes us feel happy, healthy and content. Scents are extraordinarily evocative and can bring to mind memories of childhood, places or people long gone, and their power should never be underestimated. Each area of the garden should be treated individually when it comes to introducing fragrance, but the one element they all require is shelter. The more sheltered the position, the stronger the scent will be.

Near the house

In the area immediately outside the house, the places to concentrate on are around the windows and doors, especially the ones you open regularly during the summer. Fragrant climbers are ideal for training on the walls of the house, including *Wisteria*, Chinese jasmine (*Trachelospermum*), roses (*Rosa*) and honeysuckle (*Lonicera*). The exact choice of plant, however, will be largely governed by the orientation of the house because different plants can tolerate different conditions.

Try to select the right plant for the location. For instance, if you are looking for a plant to fragrance the bedroom, choose one like honeysuckle (*Lonicera*). This produces most of its scent during the evening because it is pollinated mainly by moths, and is therefore ideal for growing near a room that is occupied mainly at night. In winter, when you may use only the main door to the house, plant a *Daphne* or *Viburnum* nearby so that you can smell it each time you go in or out. This is particularly useful if you tend not to venture into your garden a great deal during cold weather – remember, there is always a way to benefit from fragrant plants, whatever the weather. If you enjoy cooking, keep a range of your favourite herbs within easy reach of the kitchen door so that you can cut some easily and quickly, even if it is raining.

If your sitting room has doors opening onto the garden, aim for a range of plants that will provide scent throughout late spring, summer and autumn when the doors will be opened regularly. Use every option in terms of climbers, ground cover and containers to extend the season whenever possible.

Along pathways

Pathways are an essential part of the garden. They take us to important destinations such as the washing line, compost heap and dustbin, and also transport us around the different areas of planting so that we can enjoy the garden to the full. Many pathways are attractive features in themselves, but even the most dull-looking path can be enlivened with careful planting. Use an edging of fragrant, low-growing plants that can be clipped back if they start to encroach on the pathway itself – pansies (*Viola*), thyme (*Thymus*), chamomile (*Chamaemelum*), swan river daisies (*Brachycome*) and lavender (*Lavandula*) are all suitable.

*This lemon tree (*Citrus limon*) is perfectly located near french doors, so that its fragrance can be enjoyed both in the home and in the garden. You can put large containers on casters so they are easy to move.*

If you are building a pathway from scratch, you could leave planting gaps at intervals along its length so that low-growing plants can be inserted to break up any hard lines even further. However, this may not be advisable if the pathway is regularly used to carry items such as trays of food or baskets of washing, which can obscure your sight of the path.

Around sitting areas

Patios and decking may be treated in the same way as pathways, bringing the plants over the edges so that there are no hard lines on view and you get as much fragrance from the garden as possible. One of the most enchanting ways in which to enjoy fragrant plants is to turn the seating area into a scented arbour where you can sit, relax and appreciate the splendour of your garden. An arbour overhanging with scented roses (*Rosa*) is a truly romantic setting.

Near the dining area

There are many reasons for using fragrant plants around an outdoor eating area, all of which will influence the plants used. If you often dine there during the day, when you need shade from the heat of the sun, use a leafy climber such as *Wisteria*. If you use the area in the evening, then the emphasis changes to plants that have scent at that time of day, such as honeysuckle (*Lonicera*) and night-scented stock (*Matthiola bicornis*).

If you cook outdoors on a barbecue, you might need a range of fragrant and tasty herbs nearby. In the heat of the day, these smell wonderful as they release their essential oils into the air, and they are ready to use when you cook. Some plants are useful for their insect-repellent qualities. Ants, for example, dislike the scent of mint and will avoid it if they can, so low-growing pennyroyal (*Mentha pulegium*) can be used around the edge of the seating area to deter them.

Around special features

A successful garden usually has distinct areas of interest, and one of the easiest ways to achieve this is to introduce special features and focal points at carefully selected locations. This could be a statue or a water feature, for instance. A good way to use fragrance to complement special features is to build up the aroma gradually as you near the feature, so that from a distance there is just a hint of scent and, as you draw nearer, the aroma grows until it reaches its climax at the feature itself. However, try not to go overboard, since an overpowering fragrance will make it unpleasant to linger there.

The plants you choose to position around the special features in your garden should be those with the fragrance you most enjoy. Obviously, focal points such as a water feature will have a more limited number of plants to choose from, but there are still enough to suit most tastes, from the many strikingly beautiful waterlilies to pretty cinnamon-scented sweet flag (*Acorus calamus*). Remember, too, that you can plant fragrant flowers in the area around the water feature, though you need to make sure that the different scents complement one another.

Scent during the evening

There is nothing nicer than making the most of a warm summer's evening by relaxing in the garden and, if the air can be perfumed as well, so much the better. There are many plants that are fragrant throughout daylight hours, but some plants are scented only in the evening because they are pollinated by night-flying insects such as moths.

The pretty pink and white flowers of Lilium speciosum *release a sweet fragrance in the evening, perfect for dining and seating areas.*

Varieties of honeysuckle (*Lonicera*), *Nicotiana*, sweet mignonette (*Reseda odorata*), night-scented stock (*Matthiola bicornis*), *Mirabilis jalapa*, lilies (*Lilium*), *Phlox*, evening primrose (*Oenothera*), roses (*Rosa*) and sweet rocket (*Hesperis*) all smell delightful during the evening. Use them near open windows and doors, and near the outdoor dining or sitting areas.

Fragrant plants for containers

The great attraction of growing fragrant plants in containers is that they are movable, so you can position them wherever they will give the best effect. If you have steps leading to a door, smaller containers can be placed on each side at the base of the steps so that the scent accompanies you as you climb. More scented plants can be placed in containers at the doorway itself.

On the patio or sitting area, containers can be moved to the fore as they come into flower and retired to the back as they fade, so you have constant interest and fragrance. They can be moved nearer to the dining area if you are entertaining, or placed near a window if the weather is not warm enough to sit outside.

To make moving a large container easier, you can fit small casters to the base before you plant it up. Then it can be moved into position quickly and easily. This will allow you to use taller plants as a mobile screen – near the dining area, for instance – to give privacy. Climbing plants grown on a tripod, wigwam or obelisk are effective for this, as are small trees. Almost any plant will grow in a container as long as it is well cared for. Even fruit trees such as apples (*Malus*) are suitable as long as you select a variety grown on a dwarfing rootstock to limit the growth rate and you remember to water, feed and repot it regularly.

Planting for fragrance all-year-round

There are plants in flower during each month of the year, even in the depths of winter – all you have to do is seek them out. Surprisingly, the ones that flower in winter often have a stronger fragrance than those that flower in summer. This is because a shortage of pollinating insects means that the plant has to work harder to attract them. However, the winter-flowering types can often look quite dull during the rest of the year, so plant them in a position where the scent can be easily appreciated in winter (close to a path), yet with a colourful companion for interest during the rest of the year. Alternatively, you could plant a small *Clematis texensis* to grow through a winter-flowering shrub such as *Viburnum farreri*, for instance, so that it flowers in the late summer, giving an extra season of interest.

Indoor fragrance

Plants can provide fragrance indoors in several ways. Dried flowers, petals and leaves can be used in formal arrangements and bowls of potpourri (see page 30); cut flowers look wonderful in a vase or formal arrangement; and fragrant flowering plants may be grown in the house or conservatory. Each of these looks attractive and fills the room with natural fragrance, although it is important to be aware that some sweet, cloying fragrances can become overpowering and are best used in larger, cooler areas of the house than in confined warm ones.

Climbers have been trained up the walls of this house to bring fragrance right to the bedroom window – a perfect way to wake up.

chapter three

3

THE FRAGRANT GARDEN IN SPRING THE FRAGRANT GARDEN IN SPRING THE FRAGRANT GARDEN IN SPRING THE FRAGRANT GARDEN IN SPRING...

Plants for spring

Spring is the time of year when the garden comes to life. Within just a few weeks, it is transformed from a seemingly lifeless area into one that is bursting with colour and energy. The plants vie with one another to produce the best show of flowers and new leaves, and the air is heavy with perfume and the drone of bees. There is a wide variety of plants that provide spring fragrance and, as a result, it is more difficult to know what to leave out of your planting design than what to put into it. Two of the most dramatic groups at this time are trees, due their larger size, and bulbs, because of their beautiful shapes and colours. The choice of tree will depend on the size of your garden, while the range of spring-flowering fragrant bulbs is staggering.

Large trees

Trees provide privacy, improve the atmosphere and take the garden into the third dimension of height. Large gardens can cope with large trees such as the horse chestnut (*Aesculus hippocastanum*), which has small, sweetly fragrant flowers in candle-like clusters. The medium-sized garden has the widest range of choice, with trees like *Malus hupehensis*, *Prunus* x *yedoensis* and *Magnolia* x *soulangeana*, all of which provide a wonderful display during the early part of the new season.

Small trees

Small gardens or areas such as terraces where the plants may be confined to containers require a more careful choice of tree. *Laburnum* x *watereri* 'Vossii' and *Arbutus andrachne* grow into attractive small trees; both prefer to be planted in the ground. For the container, fruit trees grown on dwarf rootstocks are an ideal means of combining fragrance in spring with fruit later in the year. Apples (*Malus*) growing on a dwarf rootstock such as M27 will do well in containers. Delicately scented small varieties of peach (*Prunus persica*), apricot (*Prunus armeniaca*) and nectarine (*Prunus persica nectarina*) are also suitable for container growing.

Bulbs for outdoor fragrance

You can colour coordinate your borders or pots, or opt for a riot of different shades. Sizes range from just 3cm (1in) high to 50cm (20in), so choose varieties that will be in scale with their surroundings. Keep some of the smaller ones in attractive pots and place them in full view when the flowers are at their best, then move them to a quiet corner of the garden as they fade to allow them to die down. Daffodils and other members of the *Narcissus* family are highly fragrant and have the advantage that the flowers can be picked and brought indoors.

Bulbs for indoor fragrance

One of the most popular bulbs for indoor fragrance is *Hyacinthus*, which is available in white and shades of red, blue, yellow and orange. Hyacinths can be bought as dormant 'forced' bulbs (prepared for early flowering) in autumn and grown in a cool, dark place over the winter, ready for flowering in spring, or bought in spring as pre-grown plants just before flowering. You can combine several bulbs together in a large container for a dramatic and more fragrant effect.

Spring-flowering Magnolia x soulangeana *'Rustica Rubra', with its creamy pink flowers and strong scent, is ideal for a medium-sized garden.*

Spring weather and its effects

At this time of year the weather can be deceptive, with high daytime temperatures and bright sunlight that encourage rapid plant growth, followed by plunging night temperatures and late frosts that can scorch it off again. Frosts can catch out even experienced gardeners, particularly in late spring when it is easy to be deceived by the warm days into believing the cold weather has passed. It is important to be aware that this can cause problems and to take precautions to avoid losing shoot tips, leaves or even whole plants to the chill (see Windbreaks, page 55, and Using a Cloche, page 57). Sheltering plants from the wind helps to emphasise their fragrance because the essential oils are not blown away. The flowers also last longer when they are not subject to strong winds that shatter the blooms.

The strawberry tree (Arbutus andrachne) *is perfect for a small garden. Named for its strawberry-like fruits that appear in autumn, it also produces delicate honey-scented white flowers in spring.*

Jobs for spring

Spring is one of the busiest times of the gardener's year. In fact, so much needs doing that it can be hard to decide where to start. Everything seems to need attention during spring, from tiny new seedlings that require regular watering and protection from cold winds to full-grown plants that need feeding and pruning in order to flower well. You should also spend time controlling the growth of weeds. They seem to grow overnight at this time of year and the battle to curb them is constant. This is the time to assess whether to apply a thick mulch to control weeds or plant densely leaved, ground-covering plants instead. You will need to prioritise the various jobs that are required, giving attention to whichever is the most urgent at any particular time.

Feeding

To ensure that there are nutrients in the soil when the roots begin to search for them, feed plants during spring. This will provide the plants with the minerals they need to grow, flower and fruit as well as withstand attack by pests or disease. The top priority is to give them a feed of general fertiliser. The winter rain will have washed whatever nutrients were in the soil the previous year down beyond the reach of most roots, so the nutrients need to be replaced if the plants are to perform well. The danger of not feeding is cumulative rather than immediate, so although there is no noticeable effect if you do not feed plants during spring, the growth will gradually slow and the flowers reduce in size.

Plants need a range of nutrients to grow well, from the main elements of nitrogen (N), phosphorus (P) and potassium (K) to minor trace elements including magnesium and copper. On the fertiliser bag or container, the three main elements are given in a ratio to one other, because each has a different part to play in plant growth and may be needed at a different time of year. In basic terms, plants need nitrogen for shoots (healthy top growth, larger leaves), phosphorus for roots and potassium for fruits and flowers. Most plants benefit from more nitrogen and phosphorus in spring when they are growing quickly, but less in summer, when the emphasis changes to potassium. For the largest and most fragrant flowers, increased potassium should be applied from late spring onwards. If scented foliage is more important to you, use a high nitrogen feed during late spring.

Pruning

Plants need to be pruned in order to flower well. If you are hesitant about which shrubs to prune and when to do so, aim to prune after flowering so that the plant has a full year to recover, ready for flowering again the following year. By removing the shoot that has flowered, you will encourage the plant to produce new replacement stems that will flower in years to come.

Weed control

The battle against weeds is never-ending in the garden, especially in spring when their rate of growth seems to outstrip everything else. However, there are ways of reducing the amount of time you have to spend pulling them out. Like any other seedlings, they need light to grow, so smothering the soil will help. You can

Feeding plants is important if you are to achieve a good show of healthy flowers. Concentrate on providing nitrogen and phosphorus in the spring.

use a mulch, such as shredded bark, but in a scented garden you should seek out densely leaved, ground-covering plants instead. These will shade the soil and block the light as well as emit fragrance from their flowers and/or foliage if you choose the right variety, such as a low-growing rose (*Rosa*) or thyme (*Thymus*).

Dwarf shrubs such as this Daphne retusa *can be used as ground cover to help control weeds as well as provide fragrance.*

Windbreaks

The wind can be both cold and strong in spring, and delicate new leaves and shoots are vulnerable to it. Both are at their most vulnerable in spring, before they have had a chance to toughen up, and a period of strong wind can cause extensive damage. The cells are chilled and dried, resulting in an effect known as scorching because that is exactly what it resembles.

Use windbreaks to help make sure that tender young plants are kept sufficiently warm. These may be temporary or movable, such as plastic mesh, horticultural fleece or a cloche, or permanent. The most permanent is a wall, but the danger of a solid barrier is that it diverts the wind upwards, causing it to swirl. This turbulence can produce more damage to the plants on the other side of the wall than the wind would have done. A permeable material that allows some of the wind to filter through is more effective, such as plastic mesh, woven wooden fencing, willow hurdles or living hedges. All of these will have a screening effect, giving privacy as well as less wind disturbance. In a small garden, a screening plant such as bamboo can be planted in a container with wheels, to be moved around the garden to the places where it is most useful at any particular time.

Propagation & planting

Spring is the busiest time of year for seed propagation because this is the time when light levels begin to increase and temperatures rise. If you are planning a display of annual colour and fragrance, it is important to sow the seed now because the young plants need to grow and mature in time to produce the flowers. With practice, it is possible to sow successive batches of seed so that you get flowers throughout the summer rather than in one brief display. Soft-tip cuttings can be taken from plants such as geranium (*Pelargonium*) in order to increase your stocks. Both seedlings and cuttings need repotting regularly to keep them growing strongly, and they need protecting from inclement weather, which can kill the plants or encourage disease.

Seedlings and cuttings

Sow seeds at this time of year, aiming for a range of flowering times so that you have a strong display throughout the season. A greenhouse is ideal for this and can make both indoor and outdoor gardening easier. If you are planning a summer display, you can bulk up your plant numbers by taking cuttings from existing plants or new ones as they grow in the greenhouse.

If the greenhouse is heated, you can use it to protect any plants that will be affected by frost and to hurry plants along a little to reduce any gaps in the planned displays throughout the colder months of the year. If you do not have a greenhouse and are planting seeds in the open, cover them with individual or tunnel cloches overnight and during bad weather (see below).

Resting plants

While the new season's seedlings and cuttings are growing on the shelving in the greenhouse, use the space on the floor below to allow indoor plants to rest and recuperate after their displays have finished. Bulbs look less than attractive while their foliage dies down, but they need somewhere to replenish their energy and prepare for the next season, and a corner of a greenhouse or cold frame is ideal.

Planting out

After germination, seedlings need care to ensure they continue to grow and do not succumb to pests, disease or the weather. If they are in trays or pots, you need to acclimatise them as they get bigger by exposing them to the elements during the day and returning them to a protected environment overnight until the weather is warm enough to leave them outside all the time. They may need overnight protection for some time, so do not be tempted by a few warm days into putting them in their final planting position until all danger of late frost has passed.

Alternatively, place the seedlings in an unheated greenhouse or cold frame. This is warmer than outdoors but cooler than indoors, making it an ideal 'halfway house' for acclimatising plants. The drawback is that you could be caught out by a rogue frost and lose a valued plant. Once the seedlings have been successfully acclimatised, plant them out into a well-prepared plot so that they can carry on growing to maturity.

You can take soft-tip cuttings from geraniums (Pelargonium) during the spring. Repot the cuttings regularly to ensure strong growth.

Spring is the busiest time of year for sowing seeds and nurturing young seedlings. The rewards in the summer will be well worth the effort.

Feeding young plants

You should incorporate a suitable feed into the ground as you plant out seedlings and cuttings, or apply a liquid fertiliser once the plants are growing strongly (this is particularly important if you are sowing seed directly into its final position). Liquid feeds are easy and convenient because they can be applied when the plants are watered. Remember to do this regularly because some is always washed away through the soil.

Sheltering young plants

The weather can have a profound effect on plant growth and a windbreak may be the difference between life and death for a young plant. If your garden is exposed, it makes sense to keep some protection at hand that can be put into place around the plants in the event of a period of bad weather. A temporary windbreak, such as netting around the immediate area, may be sufficient in spring when the young seedlings are planted out. If the garden is windswept throughout the year, it may be worth considering a permanent solution (see Windbreaks, page 53).

Using a cloche

A cloche is a small, often portable structure that can be placed over a plant to protect it from the weather. It may be plastic or glass and should allow the maximum amount of light to reach the plant. Cloches can also be used for night protection by placing the structure over the plant as the temperatures fall and removing it in the morning as they rise again. Protecting the plant encourages it to grow more quickly than its exposed counterparts, producing its flowers earlier and with less damage. Used on bare earth before planting, the cloche can warm the soil more quickly than if it were unprotected, allowing earlier planting. Plastic sheets can be used as a tunnel to cover a much larger area for planting a whole row.

Pruning

Some of the most fragrant plants produce their flowers at the most unlikely time of year. During the chilly winter season, a brief period of winter sunshine can produce a burst of blooms with a very strong fragrance. It is important that you prune these plants in spring immediately after flowering to ensure a strong display of flowers in future years.

WHAT YOU NEED
Tools: Secateurs; pruning saw; garden fork

Plants such as the shrubby honeysuckles are capable of producing flowers from late autumn until late winter (*Lonicera standishii*) and mid-winter until mid-spring (*L. fragrantissima* and *L.* x *purpusii*). These plants produce their flowering wood during the current growing season and very rarely flower on two-year-old wood. They must therefore be pruned to ensure a fresh supply of flowering shoots in years to come.

The best time to do this is in spring immediately after flowering, just as the old flowers are fading. By cutting off the growths that are carrying the fading flowers, you can be certain that the right shoots are being removed. This will create the space needed for future flowering wood. As the plant matures, some of the oldest stems will need to be removed completely to encourage a more open habit and create space in the centre of the shrub for new shoots to grow from the base. Each year, around 25 per cent of the oldest stems should be cut down to their base.

Tip: Some shrubs, such as *Daphne bholua*, *Jasminum nudiflorum*, *Mahonia* x *media*, *Sarcococca humilis*, *Viburnum* x *bodnantense* and the honeysuckles mentioned above, naturally produce long branches that often arch over to touch the ground. They may begin to form roots where they touch the soil, producing new shrubs by a process known as 'simple layering'. It is important that you do not prune these shoots until the new plant has had the chance to develop a good root system.

Start by cutting out any dead, dying, diseased or damaged stems using a pair of secateurs. Then cut out those shoots that have old fading flowers on them. Cut them back to a strong pair of buds close to the main stem.

Remove about 25 per cent of the oldest shoots from the plant. Cut as close to ground level as possible. These are usually the thicker stems with darker coloured bark. For the thickest, it is easier to use a pruning saw than secateurs.

If possible, leave strong young shoots growing from the centre of the plant undamaged. These will become replacements for the older growth that is being removed.

Where shoots have arched over and rooted into the ground (simple layering), gently ease the roots out of the ground using a garden fork. These new plants can be transferred to sites in other parts of the garden if required.

Prune back any new shoots that are long and straggly by one-third of their total length from the tip. Always prune to a pair of healthy buds because this promotes rapid healing of the pruning cuts and reduces the chance of these shoots dying.

Any discarded branches and shoots should be taken away for shredding or burning. Remove any small twigs or branches left lying on the ground around the plant to help prevent disease from spreading into the shrub.

Fragrant ground cover

It is possible to have a fragrant garden that is also low-maintenance. Many of the more modern varieties of 'ground cover' roses have a low, spreading habit as well as scented blooms. This means that they will eventually form a dense leaf canopy, providing a living mulch of plants that will suppress many of the weeds encountered in the garden as well as creating a fragrant carpet.

WHAT YOU NEED
Tools: Spade; knife; wheelbarrow; garden fork
Materials: Pot-grown roses; plastic membrane; organic mulch

For ground-cover plants to work effectively, their site must be well-prepared and free from all traces of perennial weeds. This will give the newly introduced plants the best possible start. Using ground-cover roses in conjunction with a mulch will give even more effective cover and can also be used for aesthetic effect. Planting roses through membrane sheeting covered with a layer of deep brown bark nuggets or shredded wood fibre, for example, can set up a striking contrast between the different shades of green foliage and the texture of the mulch.

There are three main reasons for covering the sheeting: weighing down the sheeting will prevent it from flapping in the wind; plastic sheeting looks unsightly; and plastic biodegrades quickly when exposed to sunlight. The main purpose of the mulch is to control the weeds until the new plants become established, and to reduce the need for watering by trapping moisture in the soil and preventing water loss through evaporation from the soil surface. Usually, the only maintenance required is to keep dead-heading the roses to ensure that a continuous supply of sweetly scented flowers is produced throughout the growing season.

> **Tip:** Lightly trim ground-cover roses with a hedge trimmer immediately after flowering. You should remove approximately the top third of the growth. This will encourage another flush of flowers.

Start by marking out where each plant is going to be positioned, or stand the plants (in their containers) in their intended positions. This will give a better idea of how the bed will look when it has been planted.

Remove the plants and dig a planting hole large enough to accommodate the whole root system, keeping the top-soil and sub-soil separate. Spread the sub-soil over the surface of the bed and keep the top-soil close to the planting hole.

Place a sheet of heavy gauge woven plastic membrane over the bed and seal the edges by tucking them in, at least 15cm (6in) deep, and stretching the sheeting as tight as possible.

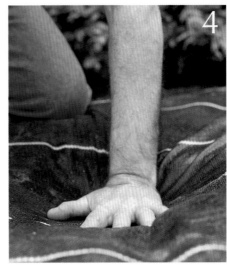

Press down gently onto the membrane to find the location of the planting holes and cut a cross in the sheeting at the point where each plant is to be placed.

Fold back the flaps of the cross to reveal the planting hole beneath. Holding the plant by its stem or leaves, gently remove it from the container. Position the plant in the planting hole, pull the soil back into the hole around the plant, and firm gently into place.

Immediately after planting, fold the plastic flaps back into position around the base of the plant. Hide the sheeting by covering it with a layer of organic material, such as bark chippings or wood chips, and spread them evenly over the sheeting.

Fragrance indoors

The first few weeks of spring can seem dull in the garden, with leafless trees taking on a grey cast and grass turning a drab grey-green. Even if your garden has colour and interest in the late winter/early spring period, the weather may be too cold for you to spend much time outside appreciating it. This is therefore a good time to ensure that you have plenty of colour and fragrance indoors. This will cheer you up and remind you that the warmer days of late spring and summer really are just around the corner.

Bulbs

One of the easiest ways to create indoor colour is with bulbs, which can be chosen to flower in succession from mid-winter until late spring. Bulbs are small, conveniently packaged and not overly demanding of attention. In return for compost and regular water, they provide colourful flowers that fill the house with natural fragrance. You can choose the colour and amount of fragrance they release to suit you and your home. Miniature *Narcissus* such as 'Tête-à-Tête' reach about 20cm (8in) high and have a sweet, delicate perfume. Taller varieties such as 'Paper White' (*N. papyraceus*) reach 45cm (18in) and their scent is powerful. Hyacinths (*Hyacinthus*) are highly scented and may need staking as they open because the weight of the flower may pull the stem over.

Bulbs take 10–12 weeks to develop and flower, so plant them in autumn to provide colour for early spring. Choose an attractive container and plant them in bulb compost. Keep the compost thoroughly moist but not wet. Once the flowers begin to open, apply a general liquid fertiliser every fortnight when you are watering. As the flowers die, remove them to prevent the plant from wasting energy by setting seed. Leave the flower stem intact so that it and the leaves can die down naturally and replenish the bulb ready for the following year. Continue watering and feeding until the foliage has died right back, then let the bulb dry out. Store it until the following year or plant it in the garden to provide colour for years to come.

Growing conditions

All bulbs and indoor plants have a range of conditions in which they will thrive, and another in which they can survive. Different parts of the house offer very different conditions, and the levels of light, heat and humidity vary considerably. Plants share a common dislike of draughts and extremes of temperature, but otherwise have different growing requirements.

Light

Light levels are important, and they drop quickly as you move away from the window. Plants with white- or yellow-variegated leaves need the highest levels, and those with dark green leaves can tolerate the deepest shade. By selecting the variety to suit the position, it is possible to find a plant for all but the darkest corner.

If the weather is still too cold in spring to spend much time in the garden, bring cut flowers into the home to enjoy their fragrance.

Narcissus *are available in many different forms, from extravagant double-flowered varieties to simple trumpet-shaped blooms. Plant bulbs of different varieties that will flower in succession throughout the spring.*

Heat

Plants that prefer warm conditions, such as *Gardenia* and *Hoya*, are ideal for kitchens and bathrooms, whereas those needing a cooler environment, such as *Jasminum* and *Stephanotis*, may suit the bedroom. If the plant is on the windowsill during winter, move it into the main part of the room overnight because the temperature behind closed curtains can be 10°C (18°F) colder than inside and the plant can suffer cold damage if it is left there.

Humidity

Humidity can be increased around plants such as *Citrus* and *Gardenia* by standing the pot on a saucer of gravel and water. The water will evaporate up the pot, creating moist conditions around the leaves. Grouping plants together helps to trap this moisture and create a micro-environment. The roots of the plant must not be allowed to stand in the water or they will rot.

Conservatories

A conservatory offers many possibilities for growing plants as it provides extra space and high light levels. Many indoor plants thrive in these conditions, like the strongly fragrant white jasmine (*Jasminum polyanthum*), which is tolerant of cooler temperatures. Other plants may not survive over winter unless the conservatory is heated, including aromatic plants such as *Citrus* (oranges and lemons). These are ideal for large conservatories where their aromatic foliage can provide respite from the sun.

Forcing bulbs

Many of the hardy bulbs that bloom outdoors during late winter and spring can be tempted into flowering indoors many weeks earlier by using specially prepared bulbs. These bulbs are known as 'forced' bulbs and they can provide an excellent display of indoor colour and fragrance during the colder months when gardening outdoors may be difficult.

WHAT YOU NEED
Materials: Compost; plant pots; bulbs; straw, newspaper or sand; bulb bowls; grit or sphagnum moss; high-potassium fertiliser; stakes and string (for tall-stemmed flowers)

Forced bulbs have been given special treatment to advance their development and shorten their growing season. This involves the bulb grower lifting the bulbs from the field and storing them for a period of time in storage sheds at temperatures of 25–35°C (77–95°F) to speed up the development of the flower bud. The second stage of treatment is a period of about six weeks' storage at a much lower temperature, usually below 10°C (50°F). This is done to mimic the winter cold that the bulbs would experience naturally so that they will start into growth earlier than normal. All of this preparation is carried out before the bulbs are offered for sale in garden centres and shops.

Hyacinths have been used in this project. However, the difficulty with forcing hyacinths of mixed colours is that no two cultivars grow at exactly the same rate, and there is nothing more disappointing than having the flowers open at different times rather than simultaneously. To combat this problem, grow each colour separately so that you can slow down or advance its development to keep the growth of each batch balanced with the others. Plant the bulbs for forcing in late summer or early autumn, keeping bulbs of the same cultivar together.

Tip: Keep the bulbs well watered to maintain a good show of flowers. After flowering, remove the flower head (but leave the green flower stem) and put the bowl in a cool place. Continue to feed and water the bulbs until they are ready to be planted outdoors in April.

Sprinkle a layer of compost in the bottom of the pot and insert the bulb; make sure it does not touch the sides of the pot. Fill in the spaces between the pot rim and the bulb with compost, and firm it gently so that it is 1cm (½in) below the rim of the container to allow for watering.

Immediately after potting your bulbs, you need to give them a cold period for 8–10 weeks. This can be achieved by placing them in a cool garage or dry shed, covered with moist straw, sand or shredded newspaper.

Alternatively, place the pots of bulbs in a cold frame. Cover with straw, sand or shredded newspaper and wet them thoroughly (this is known as plunging). Keeping the bulbs moist helps to lower the temperature.

When the flower spike is about 5cm (2in) high, bring the pots indoors and place them in a cool, shaded place at 10°C (50°F) for about a week, during which time the shoots will turn green.

Knock the individual bulbs out of their pots and plant them into bulb bowls. Place a layer of grit or sphagnum moss over the surface of the compost to hold in the moisture. Feed the bulbs every seven days with a high-potassium fertiliser.

Keep the bowls in a well-lit position in a temperature of 15–17°C (59–63°F). Turn the bowls every day so that bulbs grow evenly and do not lean towards the light. Tie the flower stems of taller cultivars to stakes if they require support.

TREES

KEY INFORMATION

H: The average height the plant can reach

S: The average spread the plant can achieve

Sun/partial shade/shade: The position the plant prefers

Well-drained/moderate/moist: How much water the plant needs

Acid/alkaline/neutral/any: The plant's preferred soil type

Z1 to Z10: The minimum winter temperature (zone) the plant can withstand

Zone 1: below –46°C (below –50°F)
Zone 2: –46 to –40°C (–50 to –40°F)
Zone 3: –40 to –34°C (–40 to –30°F)
Zone 4: –34 to –29°C (–30 to –20°F)
Zone 5: –29 to –23°C (–20 to –10°F)
Zone 6: –23 to –18°C (–10 to 0°F)
Zone 7: –18 to –12°C (0 to 10°F)
Zone 8: –12 to –7°C (10 to 20°F)
Zone 9: –7 to –1°C (20 to 30°F)
Zone 10: –1 to 4°C (30 to 40°F)

Acacia longifolia
H 15m (46ft) S 8m (26ft)
Sun
Moderate
Acid/neutral Z8

This Australian native, commonly called the Sydney golden wattle, grows to become a small tree or large evergreen shrub with an open habit. The mid-green flattened modified leaves (called phyllodes) are strap-like or lance-shaped, reaching up to 15cm (6in) long with a slender, curved tip. In spring, fragrant deep-yellow cylindrical flower heads up to 7cm (3in) long and 1cm (½in) across are produced on anything from 1 to 3 spikes. Acacias resent severe pruning and will often die back. Propagate by sowing seed into pots and placing them in a heated case in spring or by taking semi-ripe tip cuttings in summer.

Laburnum x ***watereri* 'Vossii'**
H 10m (32ft) S 8m (26ft)
Sun
Moderate
Any Z6

The golden rain tree is a popular deciduous flowering tree with a slightly erect habit and grey-green branches. The grey-green leaves are made up of three small oval-shaped leaflets that are glossy on the upper surface and paler on the underside. During spring, large quantities of long, hanging clusters of golden yellow, pea-like flowers with a faint scent of freesia are produced. These are followed by small grey-brown pods that disperse poisonous black seeds in autumn. This plant will grow in a wide range of soils but has a brittle root system and must be permanently staked. Propagate by budding or grafting.

Magnolia kobus
H 12m (39ft) S 10m (32ft)
Sun/partial shade
Moderate/moist
Any Z5

A native of Japan, this is an early-flowering deciduous magnolia that develops into a broadly conical-shaped tree. The aromatic leaves are oval in shape and a mid-green colour, sometimes with a puckered edge when they first emerge.
In early spring, the tree becomes covered in large, strongly scented, goblet-shaped blooms that open to form a 'cup and saucer'-shaped flower. They are white and sometimes flushed with pink at the base of each petal. Propagate by layering in spring, taking semi-ripe cuttings in summer or sowing seed as soon as it is ripe.

Magnolia x _soulangeana_
H 7m (23ft) S 6m (20ft)
Sun/partial shade
Moderate
Acid/neutral Z5

This beautiful deciduous hybrid magnolia grows to form an architectural, wide-spreading tree. In spring, it becomes covered in large goblet-shaped blooms that resemble a waterlily flower when they are fully open. They may be white or light pink through darker shades of pink to violet-purple, and are lightly lemon-scented. The leaves, which appear as the flowers die off, are elliptical in shape and a glossy dark green in colour, sometimes lightly tinted with bronze when they are young. The cultivar 'Alba Superba' has strongly scented flowers. Propagate by layering in spring.

Prunus laurocerasus
H 8m (26ft) S 10m (32ft)
Sun
Moderate
Any Z7

Commonly called the cherry laurel, this dense, bushy small tree or large shrub forms into a framework of arching, spreading branches. It has evergreen elliptical leaves that are a glossy dark green above and paler on the underside. It is a relative of the cherry and is much valued for its profusion of spring flowers, which are creamy white and heavily scented, appearing on spikes through the canopy of evergreen leaves. The flowers are followed by red cherry-like fruits that turn black as they become fully ripe. Propagate by taking semi-ripe heel cuttings in summer and autumn.

SHRUBS

Corylopsis sinensis
H 4m (12ft) S 4m (12ft)
Partial shade
Moderate
Acid/neutral Z6

This beautiful, deciduous flowering
shrub has slender stems and a
dense, branching habit. In spring,
it produces drooping strands of
lemon-yellow flowers, which are
highly fragrant and appear before
the leaves have opened. The leaves
are broadly-oval shaped with bristle-
like teeth along the margins. When
they appear, the new leaves are
dark-green on their upper surface
and bluish-green underneath. The
delicate flowers may be damaged
by late spring frosts. Propagate by
taking softwood cuttings in summer
or by sowing seed in a cold frame in
the autumn.

Cytisus x _kewensis_
H 60cm (2ft) S 1.5m (5ft)
Sun
Moderate
Any Z6

Raised at London's Kew Gardens
in 1891, this low-growing,
sprawling deciduous shrub has
remained popular ever since. In
spring, cascades of sweetly scented,
creamy yellow, sweet pea-shaped
blooms are produced that cover the
entire bush and obscure the stems
and leaves. The mid-green leaves are
small, strap-like and covered with
very fine hairs. This plant resents
being moved and vigorous pruning.
Propagate by taking semi-ripe heel
cuttings in summer.

Cytisus multiflorus
H 3m (10ft) S 2.5m (8ft)
Sun
Moderate
Any Z6

Commonly known as the Portuguese
broom, this attractive sprawling
deciduous shrub grows upright at
first before developing an open,
spreading habit. In spring, it is
covered with creamy white, sweet
pea-shaped blooms which have a
sweet fragrance. The strap-like
leaves are mid-green in colour and
sparsely arranged along the thin,
lax, twiggy green stems. It does not
respond well to being moved or to
hard pruning. Propagate by taking
semi-ripe heel cuttings in summer.

SHRUBS

Daphne mezereum
H 1.2m (4ft) S 1m (3ft)
Sun/partial shade
Moderate
Neutral Z4

Originating from Europe and central Asia, this slow-growing deciduous shrub has an upright habit and dull, pale green to grey-green leaves that are about 13cm (5in) long. It produces a spectacular display of intensely fragrant flowers in late winter and early spring, long before the leaves emerge. The flowers are pinkish-purple, up to 6mm (¼in) long and carried in clusters of 2–5 blooms, followed by spherical, fleshy red fruits. Prune only to remove dead or damaged wood and move as little as possible because it resents disturbance. Propagate by taking semi-ripe cuttings in summer.

Euphorbia mellifera
H 2m (7ft) S 2.5m (8ft)
Sun
Well-drained/moderate
Any Z10

Originating from Madeira and commonly called the honey spurge, this rounded evergreen shrub has stout stems and dark green, strap-like leaves up to 20cm (8in) long, with a prominent rib along the centre. In late spring, an assembly of large brown bracts (modified leaves often mistaken for flowers) are carried on the tip of each stem and produce a strong scent of honey. These are followed by pea-like fruits in late summer. Propagate by sowing seed in a cold frame as soon as it is ripe or by taking semi-ripe tip cuttings in late spring or early summer.

Mahonia aquifolium
H 1.2m (4ft) S 1.2m (4ft)
Sun/partial shade
Moderate
Any Z5

Commonly known as the Oregon grape, this tough evergreen shrub has a spreading, suckering habit and is useful as ground cover or under trees in a woodland planting. The glossy dark green leaves are divided into up to nine leaflets that have bright crimson edges in winter. In spring, sweetly scented yellow flowers are produced in dense clusters on the shoot tips. Attractive cultivars include M. a. 'Atropurpurea' (rich red-purple leaves in winter) and M. a. 'Apollo' (low growing with golden yellow flowers). Prune only to maintain the shape and health of the plant. Propagate by taking semi-ripe cuttings in late summer or suckers in autumn.

SHRUBS

Osmanthus x burkwoodii
H 3m (10ft) S 3m (10ft)
Sun/partial shade
Moderate
Any Z6

This plant is a hybrid between
O. decorus and *O. delavayi*.
It is a slow-growing evergreen shrub
with a dense, rounded habit, often
spreading with age. The glossy
dark green leaves have a leathery
texture and are broadly elliptical
in shape, about 5cm (2in) long,
with a slightly toothed margin. In
mid- to late spring, small, tubular
fragrant flowers are produced in
small clusters in the axils of the
leaves and stem but, being a hybrid
plant, it very rarely produces fruits.
Propagate by sowing seed in a cold
frame as soon as it is ripe or by
taking semi-ripe cuttings in summer.

Osmanthus delavayi
H 2m (7ft) S 2m (7ft)
Sun/partial shade
Moderate
Any Z7

This rounded evergreen shrub has
arching branches and is ideal for
a border or under light tree cover.
The leathery dark green leaves have
toothed edges and remain glossy
throughout the year. In late spring,
the strongly fragrant white flowers
appear in clusters along the shoots,
each tubular in shape, flaring out
into four lobes. The flowers are
followed by blue-black fruits. If
necessary, prune after flowering to
remove dead or damaged wood,
although it will tolerate hard
pruning and may be trained against
a wall. Propagate by taking semi-
ripe cuttings in late summer or
sowing seed as soon as it is ripe.

Rhododendron cubittii
H 1.5m (5ft) S 1m (3ft)
Partial shade
Moderate
Acid Z10

Originating from northern Myanmar,
this suckering evergreen shrub is
still known by many gardeners as
an azalea. In winter, it produces
purple-brown young shoots. In
spring, it produces large quantities
of highly fragrant white to pale pink
funnel-shaped blooms. These have
deep-orange or yellow markings and
form into a rounded truss. The mid-
to dark green, broadly oval-shaped
leaves are up to 10cm (4in) long
and have a leathery texture.
Propagate by taking softwood
cuttings in early summer or sowing
seed under protection in late spring.

Rhododendron luteum
H 2.5m (8ft) S 3m (10ft)
Sun
Moderate
Acid/neutral Z5

This deciduous shrub is one of
the few scented rhododendrons
and one of the easiest to grow,
although it does prefer acidic soil.
In late spring, the large flower buds
open into long-tubed flowers that
are clear yellow and highly fragrant.
The leaves are broadly spear-
shaped, mid-green and slightly
sticky when young, changing to
shades of crimson, purple and
orange in autumn. Although quick
to establish, this plant will grow
slowly and steadily to form a large
dome shape. Propagate by taking
semi-ripe cuttings or layering in
late summer.

Syringa oblata
H 5m (16ft) S 5m (16ft)
Sun
Moderate
Any Z7

Originating from Korea, this
vigorous shrub has an erect habit
when young, changing to an open,
spreading habit with age. The
deciduous heart-shaped leaves are
tapered to a point and tinted bronze
when young, changing to a glossy
mid-green as they mature and
turning purple before falling in
autumn. In mid- to late spring,
broad spikes of highly fragrant pale
lilac flowers are produced. The only
pruning required is removal of the
dead flowers. Propagate by taking
softwood cuttings or layering in
early summer, budding in mid-
summer or grafting in winter.

Viburnum carlesii
H 2m (7ft) S 2m (7ft)
Sun/partial shade
Moderate
Any Z9

This slow-growing, densely twiggy
deciduous shrub is grown for its
beautiful, sweetly fragrant spring
flowers. These are produced before
the foliage in domed clusters at the
tips of the shoots. They are rose pink
in bud, opening to white-flushed
pink, and are followed by fruit that
ripens from red to black. The leaves
are coarse, toothed and mid-green
and often turn red before falling in
autumn. The cultivar 'Aurora' has
deep-pink buds and pink flowers,
fading to white. This is a lovely
specimen for a border or container.
Prune lightly after flowering to
maintain the shape and remove any
damaged wood. Propagate by taking
soft-tip cuttings in summer.

CLIMBERS & WALL SHRUBS

Akebia quinata
H 5m (16ft) S 5m (16ft)
Sun/partial shade
Moderate
Any Z5

The chocolate vine is a semi-evergreen twining climber with palmate leaves of mid-green, tinted bronze as they emerge. The vanilla-scented flowers appear in spring, in rich maroon to chocolate brown – hence the common name. Male and female flowers are borne within the same cluster: small male ones at the tip and larger female ones at the base. Long, purple, sausage-shaped fruits will be produced in a hot summer if there is a second plant nearby to pollinate. If necessary, prune after flowering to maintain the shape. Propagate by layering in spring, taking semi-ripe cuttings in summer or sowing seed as soon as it is ripe.

Azara dentata
H 3m (10ft) S 3m (10ft)
Sun
Well-drained/moderate
Any Z8

Originating from Chile, this evergreen shrub is a perfect choice for growing against a hot, sunny wall or in a sheltered garden. It has slender, arching branches and oval-shaped, glossy dark green leaves with a finely toothed margin, often hairy on the underside. In mid- to late spring, dense clusters of deep-yellow, sweetly scented flowers up to 5cm (2in) across are produced. Prune immediately after flowering by cutting the flower-bearing shoots back to 4–5 buds. Propagate by taking semi-ripe cuttings from the new side shoots in mid- to late summer.

***Ceanothus* 'Cascade'**
H 4m (13ft) S 4m (13ft)
Sun
Well-drained/moderate
Acid/neutral Z8

This vigorous, marginally hardy evergreen shrub has an open, wide-spreading habit. The glossy dark green leaves have a finely toothed margin and are oblong to oval in shape. The fragrant soft-blue flowers are carried in large pyramidal spikes up to 13cm (5in) long on the tips of the branches from late spring until early summer. This plant should be pruned immediately after flowering to prevent it from becoming straggly and bare in the centre. It is often grown against a wall to protect it from frost damage. Propagate by taking semi-ripe cuttings from the new side shoots in mid- to late summer.

CLIMBERS & WALL SHRUBS

Clematis armandii
H 4m (13ft) S 3m (10ft)
Sun
Moderate
Any Z6

This attractive woody climber is
one of the few evergreen clematis.
It is ideal against a wall or fence
because it needs shade over its
roots. The glossy, leathery, trifoliate
leaves are up to 15cm (6in) long
and tend to be tinted bronze as
they emerge, ageing to a rich
dark green. In early spring, fragrant,
saucer-shaped, pink-tinted white
flowers are produced in dense
clusters. 'Apple Blossom' has a
darker shading of pink on the
flowers, and 'Snowdrift' is pure
white. After flowering, prune
back to a strong pair of buds to
encourage flowering wood for the
following year. Propagate by taking
semi-ripe cuttings in late summer.

Lonicera syringantha
H 2m (7ft) S 2.5m (8ft)
Sun/shade
Moderate
Any Z4

This spring-flowering shrubby
honeysuckle is grown for its fragrant
flowers, which are arranged in pairs
and usually carried in small clusters
in the leaf joints of the branches.
The flowers are basically tubular
in shape, opening out to a broad
mouth, and are lilac-pink in colour,
often paler inside. The deciduous
leaves are broadly oblong in shape
and grey-green to deep green in
colour. They are carried in pairs
on thin, twiggy stems, gradually
developing an open, spreading
habit. Propagate by taking
hardwood cuttings of non-flowering
shoots in winter or softwood
cuttings in mid-summer.

Wisteria sinensis
H 10m (32ft) S 10m (32ft)
Sun/partial shade
Moderate
Any Z5

This wisteria is a beautiful, elegant
climbing plant, especially when
draped with its cascades of fragrant,
pea-like, white, pink, blue or mauve
flowers. These appear in late spring
on the bare branches, before the
leaves emerge. The leaves are dark
to mid-green in colour and divided
into small leaflets, and the plant
grows best in a south- or west-facing
situation. The vigorous stems will
twine in an anticlockwise direction
up a trellis or other support. The
white-flowered W. s. 'Alba' and
the white-tinged purple flowers
of W. s. 'Sierra Madre' are among
the most fragrant. Propagate by
layering, grafting or taking softwood
cuttings in summer.

PERENNIALS & BIENNIALS

Asphodeline lutea
H 1.5m (5ft) S 30cm (12in)
Sun
Well-drained/moderate
Neutral Z7

Commonly known as the king's
spear, this clump-forming perennial
plant has long, narrow, strap-like
leaves that are deeply grooved,
bluish-green in colour and
produced along the length of the
main stem and flower spike. In late
spring and early summer, dense,
tightly packed spikes of flowers up
to 20cm (8in) long are produced.
They carry large numbers of
fragrant, star-shaped, bright yellow
flowers that open progressively from
the base of the spike up to the tip.
Propagate by sowing seed into pots
as soon as it is ripe and placing
them in a cold frame or by dividing
in late summer or early autumn.

Erysimum cheiri
H 60cm (2ft) S 60cm (2ft)
Sun
Moderate
Alkaline/neutral Z7

This wallflower is an evergreen
shrub with woody stems that form a
low mound or dome of leaves. The
strap-like leaves are dark green with
a slightly paler underside and are
arranged in opposite pairs on grey-
green stems. In early spring, the
flowers are carried above the leaves
in dense spikes of flat, four-petalled
flowers. The cultivar 'Harpur Crewe'
has fragrant, double, mustard-yellow
flowers and will last about five years
before it will need replacing.
'Bowles Mauve' has small, rich
mauve blooms and silver-grey
leaves. Propagate by taking
softwood cuttings in late spring after
flowering.

Myosotis sylvatica
H 30cm (12in) S 15cm (6in)
Sun/partial shade
Moderate
Any Z5

The forget-me-not is a pretty, if
invasive, biennial that grows from
seed sown one summer to flower
the following spring. It self-seeds
easily and is ideal for mixed borders
or woodland areas where it can
spread. In a container, remove the
seed heads before any seeds are
shed. The tiny fragrant flowers are
blue, occasionally pink or white,
with a yellow or white eye. They
are borne on tall spikes with a
curled top that unfurls as the flowers
open from the base upwards over
a period of several weeks. The
smaller, compact forms, such as
'Blue Ball' and 'Snowball' (white),
are suitable as spring bedding.

PERENNIALS & BIENNIALS

Primula
H 20cm (8in) S 20cm (8in)
Sun/partial shade
Moderate
Any Z6

This large genus of plants includes
auricula, primrose and polyanthus.
All have a basal rosette of rough
leaves and wide-flaring, funnel-
shaped fragrant flowers. They are
grouped according to botanical
characteristics. *P. auricula* (auricula)
has flowers in a cluster on a stout
stem above the foliage in deep
yellow, red or purple with a yellow
centre. *P. vulgaris* (primrose) bears
solitary, pale yellow flowers on
short, slender stems amid the
foliage. *P. polyantha* (polyanthus)
hybrids have primrose-shaped
flowers in clusters on a stem
above the foliage in maroon,
red, orange, yellow, pink, white
or blue. Propagate by sowing seed
in spring or dividing in autumn.

Smilacina stellata
H 50cm (20in) S 45cm (18in)
Partial shade
Moderate/moist
Any Z3

A native of North America and
Mexico, and commonly known as
the star flower, this clump-forming,
hardy herbaceous perennial has
long, narrow, lance-shaped mid-
green leaves, slightly hairy on
the underside, emerging from a
creeping horizontal stem. From
late spring into summer, small
spikes of white, sweetly scented,
star-shaped flowers are produced
to form arching sprays on slender
green stems. This plant must
be sheltered from cold winds.
Propagate by sowing seed in
spring or autumn or by dividing
as soon as flowering has finished.

Viola cornuta
H 15cm (6in) S 40cm (16in)
Sun/partial shade
Moderate
Any Z7

The stems of this spreading
evergreen perennial violet are
flat at first and then turn upwards.
It has glossy oval-shaped leaves
with toothed edges and lightly
fragrant flowers during spring and
early summer. These are about
3.5cm (1½in) across, with five
widely separate petals of lilac to
violet. The lower petals have white
markings and thin, slightly curved
spurs. White, yellow, pink and red
forms have been bred. Ideally, it
should be positioned under other
plants in a border or in a permanent
container. Propagate by sowing seed
in spring as soon as it is ripe or by
dividing established clumps in
spring (after flowering) or autumn.

BULBS, CORMS & RHIZOMES

Convallaria majalis
H 23cm (9in) S 30cm (12in)
Partial shade/shade
Moderate/moist
Any Z3

The lily-of-the-valley is a beautiful
rhizomatous perennial that will
thrive in a shady spot beneath other
plants or in a container. It is low
growing and spreads as ground
cover. Pots of them can be brought
indoors to a cool room or
conservatory for flowering where
the sweet fragrance can be fully
appreciated. Broad, oval basal
leaves surround an upright flowering
stalk bearing pretty, hanging, bell-
shaped white flowers in spring.
The cultivar 'Albostriata' has white-
striped leaves, 'Flore Pleno' has
double flowers and var. rosea has
pale pink flowers. Propagate by
dividing the rhizomes in autumn,
but do not allow them to dry out.

Freesia
H 45cm (18in) S 5cm (2in)
Sun
Moderate
Any Z9

Although freesias are commonly
found as cut flowers in florist
shops, they are easy to grow from
dry corms and provide a long-
lasting display. The beautiful long,
funnel-shaped flowers are highly
fragrant, held on arching stems and
come in a wide range of colours,
including red, orange, pink, white,
blue, lilac and yellow. Double-
flowered forms are available,
although they are not generally
as fragrant as the single blooms.
The leaves are long, thin and lance-
shaped, bright green and arranged
in a flat fan shape. Propagate by
sowing seed or offsets in a
greenhouse or indoors in autumn.

Hyacinthus orientalis
H 20–30cm (8–12in) S 8cm (3in)
Sun/partial shade
Moderate
Any Z6

Hyacinths are bulbous perennials
with colourful and highly scented
waxy flowers. These are bell-shaped,
single or double, and come in
shades of white, yellow, pink,
orange, red and blue in clusters of
up to 40 on a single broad, upright
stem amid bright green, strap-like
leaves. 'Blue Jacket' (single, navy
blue), 'City of Haarlem' (single,
primrose yellow), 'Delft Blue'
(single, powder blue), 'Gipsy
Queen' (single, orange-pink),
'Hollyhock' (double, crimson)
and 'L'innocence' (single, white)
are just some of the colours
available. Propagate by removing
small offsets in summer when the
bulb is dormant. Plant with the tip
of the bulb 2–3cm (1in) below the
surface of the compost in autumn.

BULBS, CORMS & RHIZOMES

Iris unguicularis
H 45cm (18in) S 5cm (2in)
Sun/partial shade
Moderate
Alkaline/neutral Z5

This tough evergreen plant has
dark green, broadly strap-like leaves
up to 60cm (2ft) in length. The
primrose-scented flowers consist of
delicate silky petals, coloured lilac
with a yellow centre and carried
on short stems from late autumn
to early spring. There are two very
good cultivars: *I. u.* 'Mary Barnard',
which has deep violet-blue flowers
with dark veins, and the free-
flowering *I. u.* 'Walter Butt', which
has pale silvery lavender flowers.
Propagate by dividing established
plants immediately after flowering.

Narcissus
H 10–60cm (4–24in)
S 5–15cm (2–6in)
Sun/partial shade   Moderate
Any Z6

There are hundreds of varieties
of these hardy perennial spring-
flowering bulbs. They have narrow
strap-like leaves and flowers with
an inner trumpet or cup and an
outer row of petals. Flower shades
include yellow, white, orange,
cream and pink. They may be single
or clustered, with single or double
petals, and of varying lengths and
shapes of trumpet. They range from
10cm (4in) dwarf types to tall
varieties of 60cm (2ft). Dead-head
after flowering to prevent energy
from being expended on seed
formation and remove brown
foliage during mid-summer. Plant
the dormant bulbs at one-and-a-half
times their own depth in autumn.
Lift and divide every 3–5 years,
six weeks after flowering.

Tulipa
H 20–50cm (8–20in) S 10cm (4in)
Sun
Moderate
Any Z5

Tulips are perennial spring-flowering
bulbs, classified according to
botanical characteristics and time
of flowering. The flowers may
be single, double, goblet- or star-
shaped, fringed or long and slender.
Flower shades include white,
yellow, pink, red, orange and purple
to almost black. *T. kaufmanniana*
hybrids (waterlily tulip) – 'Giuseppe
Verdi' (yellow and red striped
flowers) and *T. greigii* 'Red Riding
Hood' (red flowers), for example –
are low-growing. *T. praestans* bears
clusters of up to five orange-red
flowers. Dead-head after flowering
and allow to die down. Plant new
bulbs in autumn 10–15cm (4–6in)
deep. Propagate by dividing when
the bulbs are lifted after flowering.

INDOOR PLANTS

Citrus limon
H 2m (7ft) S 1.5m (5ft)
Sun
Moderate

Citrus plants are ideal for the house or conservatory, where they produce flowers and fruit intermittently throughout the year when conditions are warm enough. The stems are spiny and the glossy deep-green leaves are oval shaped. The fragrant purple-tinged white flowers have five blunt petals and large stamens. Each fruit ripens from green to yellow, so that there will be fruit of each colour on the plant at the same time. How palatable they are depends on the variety. *C. l.* 'Variegata' has leaves that are variegated cream and fruit striped green, becoming fully yellow as they mature. Propagate by taking semi-ripe tip heel cuttings in spring or summer.

Gardenia augusta
H 45cm (18in) S 45cm (18in)
Partial shade
Moderate

This bushy evergreen shrub is grown for its large waxy flowers, which are up to 7cm (3in) across, white and intensely fragrant. They are usually double (many petalled) but also occur as semi-double (two layers of petals). The lance-shaped, dark green leaves are 5–10cm (2–4in) long, glossy and leathery. It prefers to grow in conditions of warmth and high humidity, especially while the flower buds are forming, so stand the pot on a tray of moist pebbles and mist the plant frequently. Any pruning should be done immediately after flowering, removing faded flowers and cutting back to an outward-facing bud. Propagate by taking tip cuttings in spring.

Genista falcata
H 1m (3ft) S 1.5m (5ft)
Sun
Well-drained/moderate

Originating from Spain and Portugal, this small deciduous gorse-like shrub is erect when young but develops a rounded, low spreading habit with slender drooping green branches. The branches are almost leafless, with many of the side shoots ending with sharp spines at the tips. The tough, sparse leaves are mid-green in colour and strap-like, with fine white, silky hairs produced only on the youngest shoots. The heavily scented pea-like flowers are deep golden yellow and produced in large quantities on the tips of shoots in mid- and late spring. Propagate by sowing seed in spring.

Hoya carnosa
H 5m (16ft) S 2m (7ft)
Sun
Moderate

The miniature wax plant has trailing thick, fleshy leaves and fragrant flowers. It looks attractive in a hanging basket, where the scent and the detail of the flowers can be appreciated. The stems are initially upright, arching only as they grow longer, and the dull green leaves are borne in pairs. The small flowers are deliciously fragrant and appear in clusters of up to 10 at the ends of the shoots. Each is star-shaped, with waxy white outer petals and a purple-red centre. It likes bright, indirect light, but dislikes being repotted or disturbed. Propagate by taking tip cuttings in spring or summer.

Murraya paniculata
H 5m (16ft) S 3m (10ft)
Sun
Moderate

This native of south-east Asia, known as the orange jasmine or satinwood, will ultimately grow to form a large, strongly aromatic evergreen tree or shrub, ideal for a conservatory. The dark green leaves are glossy, smooth and divided into three or more oblong leaflets, each up to 5cm (2in) long. The small fragrant white flowers are produced in densely packed terminal clusters throughout the year and are followed by oval orange-red fruit that are attractive but not edible. Propagate by sowing seed in spring or taking semi-ripe tip cuttings in summer.

Stephanotis floribunda
H 3m (10ft) S 3m (10ft)
Sun
Moderate

The Madagascar jasmine is a climbing shrub best known for its heavily scented, waxy white flowers, but it also has wonderful leathery leaves of a glossy dark green. The 3cm (1in) long flowers are borne in clusters of 10 or more, each tubular in shape and flaring out into five lobes. It needs supporting as it grows, and will look equally attractive trained against a wall in a conservatory or indoors on a small trellis or over an archway, as long as it is positioned where its fragrance can be fully appreciated. Pinch out the growing tips to encourage bushy growth. Propagate by taking tip cuttings in late spring.

THE FRAGRANT GARDEN IN SUMMER... THE FRAGRANT GARDEN IN SUMMER THE FRAGRANT GARDEN IN SUMMER THE FRAGRANT GARDEN IN SUMMER THE FRAGRANT GARDEN IN SUMMER...

chapter four

4

Plants for summer

Summer is the time to make the most of your garden and enjoy the fragrance that lingers on the warm air. Long days and warm evenings are ideal for enjoying a relaxing outdoor meal and appreciating the sights, sounds and, above all, the scent of the great outdoors. By now, established plants should be growing well and young annual seedlings should be in their final growing positions, ready to give a burst of colour as soon as they are mature enough. Many plants are at their best in the warm months of summer, in all shapes and sizes from trees right down to ground cover. Their scents are as varied as the colours of their flowers, with some being noticeably strong and others much more subtle.

Roses

The rose is one of the most popular garden plants in cultivation. Species originating from countries as diverse as China, India and France have been grown and bred over the years into the vast range of cultivars available today. Roses have long been prized for their distinctive perfume and most of the species roses we grow today have retained their fragrance. However, many of the hybrids have lost some of their scent in the effort to produce a better flower. Roses fall into one of several categories, depending on their growth habit and type of flower. As these range in size from tiny miniatures to very large shrubs, there is a rose suitable for every size of garden or for an attractive container.

- **Miniature roses**

  These come in many colours, with flowers varying from single to fully double. Their size makes them ideal for containers, but they tend not to have a strong fragrance.

- **Patio roses**

  This type of rose is a recent introduction, consisting of a miniature variety grafted onto a straight stem up to 1m (3ft) high. It is ideal for container growing.

- **Hybrid tea roses**

  These grow as bushes and have the largest flowers, usually double or semi-double, in colours ranging from blood-red through shades of pink, orange and yellow to white. When pruned regularly, they will flower throughout the summer, especially if the heads are removed as they fade.

- **Multiflora (floribunda) roses**

  This type of rose produces blooms that are similar to those of hybrid tea roses, but usually smaller and in greater profusion. Multiflora roses come in a wide range of colours and will flower throughout the summer as long as they are dead-headed.

- **Shrub (species) roses**

  Shrub roses are varied, ranging from the 1m (3ft) high, intensely spiny *Rosa rugosa* group with strongly scented single, semi-double or double flowers to large shrubs of 3m (10ft) such as the single-flowered *Rosa glauca*. Highly

Rosa 'Brother Cadfael' is one of the modern shrub roses that has been bred to combine strong fragrance with improved disease resistance.

fragrant varieties include *Rosa mundi* (*R. gallica* 'Versicolor'), with its dramatic pink- and white-striped petals. These roses have one main flowering period followed by intermittent blooms until late summer.

- **Climbing and rambling roses**

  These have long, lax stems that need to be tied to their support structure. Ramblers flower once in early summer, with multiple small blooms in clusters. Climbers flower repeatedly throughout the summer, often with progressively larger and more fragrant blooms.

Perennials

Many perennials are also at their flowering peak in summer. The *Dianthus* family includes some highly fragrant flowering pinks, such as 'Mrs Sinkins', 'Doris' and 'Gran's Favourite', which smell predominantly of cloves. *Hemerocallis citrina* and *H.* 'Hyperion' both have sweetly scented, yellow flowers and long, architectural, strap-like green leaves. Several fragrant varieties of *Hosta* flower in summer, including *H.* 'Honeybells' and 'Royal Standard', which both have a light, sweet scent. *Paeonia* 'Sarah Bernhardt', with its beautiful large, double, rich pink flowers, is one of the few peonies with a heavy fragrance.

Perennial bulbs that flower fragrantly in summer include *Galtonia candicans* and lilies (*Lilium*), which come in all sizes and colours. Most are heavily fragrant and will fill the air with perfume on a warm day. They grow well in pots and can be moved into a prominent position near a doorway or seating area or plunged into the border while they are in full bloom and then retired to a corner to die down again. Make full use of plants such as these to fill in gaps in your patio display or add colour and interest to a dull spot in the garden.

Summer weather and its effects

The bonus of the summer is the warm sunshine, giving the perfect excuse to spend time outdoors, but the heat can be too intense at times, causing discomfort to anyone sitting in it and damage to plants that cannot escape it. There are many fragrant trees (in sizes to suit the garden) and climbing plants that can be trained over a frame or wires to give shade where it is needed. This might be over the seating area or in the part of the garden that receives the hottest midday sun. Dappled shade is preferable for the plants below, as a total exclusion of the light is as bad as too much strong sunlight, so look for small-leaved plants that allow some light to pass through.

Jobs for summer

The long, warm days of summer are ideal for gardening and an evening spent outside after a day at work – especially if you work indoors in an office – is a great way to unwind. The mad energy of spring has given way to steady growth and the plants' main need now is for water. Other jobs include training and pruning plants so that you get the best growth and display of flowers possible. Since spending time in the garden during the warm summer months is such a pleasure, you may also enjoy taking on a larger project at this time, such as constructing a scented arch or fragrant seat. Another delightful summer job is harvesting, since this is the best time to select and dry fragrant leaves and foliage for use later in the year.

Watering

Plants rely on water to live, both because they need to drink their 'food' in a solution of water through their roots and because they require moisture to keep their cell structure intact. Without sufficient water, the cells begin to lose their ability to support the plant, which we see as wilting. Regular wilting causes slow, stunted growth, poor flowers and susceptibility to pest and disease attack. Plants in containers are even more vulnerable than those in the soil because their roots are unable to seek out extra moisture in the surrounding area.

All plants need regular, reliable watering, especially during dry periods, although you can help reduce moisture loss by mulching the soil surface or planting ground cover. Watering plants in the evening is a relaxing activity, but you can automate the watering system if need be. Install a timer to switch on the water supply so that it is delivered to the plants in the late evening or early morning so the water has time to soak in before the soil heats up again. If you have containers, water can be delivered directly into the pots using narrow tubing so that none is lost onto the paving.

Training

New plants that were introduced in spring need to be tied to their supports as they grow. Climbers, in particular, need to be tied in to prevent them from being damaged; frequent tying and regular training will keep them looking attractive and under control.

Pruning

Early summer is the ideal time to prune spring-flowering shrubs. Remove the shoots that have flowered as they die off. This allows the plant the maximum time to produce more shoots. Other flowering plants such as annuals should be dead-headed immediately after the first blooms have finished, to encourage secondary flowers to develop quickly.

Providing shade

South-facing conservatories can become very hot during the summer so you may need to protect the plants inside by applying shading over the glass. You can use netting that unrolls outside, blinds on the inside or thin white paint on the glass itself. South-facing windowsills in the house also become very hot, so plants should be chosen carefully for their ability to withstand the heat.

This Wisteria floribunda *should be pruned in the summer (and again in the winter) to help it develop flowering spurs for the following year.*

*Low-growing thymes (*Thymus*) can be planted in gaps among paving slabs. When stepped on, they will release a burst of fragrance.*

Harvesting

By mid-summer, your efforts will be rewarded when your plants begin to thrive. If you are growing herbs and plants with fragrant foliage for drying, now is the time to begin harvesting non-flowering stems. Gather aromatic herbs such as mint and oregano in bunches of about 10 stems, secure with an elastic band and hang them in a warm, airy spot to dry. The foliage can be used later in the year when fresh herbs are not available. Others, such as chive leaves and borage flowers, can be finely chopped and frozen in ice cubes for use in cooking or iced drinks. (See also Harvesting & drying, pages 28–31.)

Construction

Fragrance can be incorporated into the garden in many ways, so take this into consideration if you are planning to build any structures or lay any paving during the summer. Pergolas, arches and walkways are ideal for growing scented plants because they bring the fragrance up to head-level, making it stronger and easier to appreciate. Gaps can be left among new paving slabs or bricks so that low-growing plants with fragrant foliage or flowers can be introduced. This softens the harsh outline of the paving as well as giving scent, and many of the low-growing thymes will tolerate being stepped on periodically, releasing a burst of fragrant oil from their leaves.

Propagation & planting

Summer is a busy time for propagation, including sowing seeds, taking soft-tip and semi-ripe cuttings, layering and division. By now, with the danger of frost finally passed, any bedding plants and cuttings you were raising in the greenhouse or cold frame should have been moved outside. This will leave you space in the greenhouse to grow crops of tender plants such as tomatoes. The warm weather also means it is safe to plant out half-hardy annuals and autumn-flowering bulbs. In addition, many plants that need indoor protection during the colder months of the year will enjoy spending the summer outside where they can bask in the sunshine and be washed clean by gentle summer rain.

Seedlings

Sow seeds of biennials, such as sweet William (*Dianthus barbatus*), foxglove (*Digitalis*) and wallflower (*Erisymum*), ready for planting out in autumn. If large numbers of plants are required, sow the seed outdoors in drills and thin them out after germination so that the plants are 10–15cm (4–6in) apart when they are ready for transplanting. If only a few plants are needed, grow them in seed trays before transferring them to pots so that they can be grown on until ready for transplanting.

Cuttings

Take cuttings while the shoots are growing rather than flowering. Once the hormone balance within the plant shifts from growing to flowering, the cuttings take longer to root, and cuttings of flowering shoots will seldom root at all.

Soft-tip cuttings

These are taken from the tips of the growing shoots. Strip the lower third of leaves and place the cutting in a tray or pot of compost. Take soft-tip cuttings of tender perennials so that they can be overwintered indoors or in a cool greenhouse.

Semi-ripe cuttings

These are taken from growing tip or side shoots where the wood has started to harden and turn brown. Aim for 1cm (½in) of brown stem at the base of the cutting. Take semi-ripe cuttings of lavender (*Lavandula*), sage (*Salvia*) and *Helichrysum*.

Layering

Some fragrant plants that are difficult to root from cuttings, such as *Chimonanthus praecox* and *Hamamelis*, can be propagated by layering in late spring and early summer. Choose shoots that are at least one year old and bend them down so that a portion of the stem can be buried in the soil until it forms a new root system over a period of about 12–18 months. When the new roots have formed, the layer can be severed from the parent plant and transplanted to grow independently.

To make this method of propagation work more effectively, the stem connecting the parent plant to the proposed new plant must be constricted in some way, in order to convince the plant that a section of stem will die if it does not produce roots. This can be

Sweet peas (Lathyrus odoratus) *can be grown outside greenhouses and conservatories to provide fragrant shade from the summer sun.*

done by constricting the section of stem that is pulled down and covered by soil in one of three ways: by removing a narrow ring of bark; by circling the stem with tightly bound wire; or by splitting or twisting the stem. These are all methods of restricting the flow of food into the end of the layer, forcing it to root.

Division

Summer is the time to divide plants like the bearded iris (*Iris germanica* cultivars), immediately after the flowers have withered and died. Wash the roots gently and replant only the newest sections of rhizome, discarding all old or diseased sections of the plant and those pieces that have just flowered. Replant immediately and water well.

Planting out

Early summer, once the danger of late frost has finally passed, is the time to plant out half-hardy annuals that have been hardened off during the day but have been under cover at night. You should also plant autumn-flowering bulbs such as autumn crocus (*Colchicum autumnale*) into pots, borders or in the lawn to naturalise. Most of these flower without leaves, so mark the planting spot with a stone or cane to prevent inadvertent damage.

Try to avoid planting large trees and shrubs during the driest months of summer because they may not establish due to lack of moisture around the roots. If you must plant trees and shrubs in summer, sink a piece of pipe vertically down next to the roots as you refill the hole with soil, so that you can deliver water directly to where it is needed.

Greenhouses and conservatories

You may wish to move some indoor plants outside to enjoy the warm summer weather. Although they still prefer a sunny corner because cold winds will damage them, *Citrus, Bougainvillaea*, oleander (*Nerium oleander*) and *Lantana* can all stand outside. This 'rest' outside is also a good opportunity to use sprays on these plants to control pests or diseases.

Moving plants outside will also leave you space for crops of early tomatoes and tender plants such as peppers. You can shade the outside of the greenhouse or conservatory naturally with sweet peas (*Lathyrus odoratus*), which will scramble up netting without blocking too much light inside. Known as friendship plants, sweet peas actually produce more flowers the more you cut, because they do not set seed, so you can give bunches of these fragrant blooms away to family and friends.

Rose walkway

It can be a challenge to use every bit of available space in a garden, and a structure such as a rose walkway can really earn its keep by being both attractive and fragrant as well as useful. It is an ideal way to link one area of the garden with another all year round, as well as provide shade and shelter during the summer months when the plants are in full growth.

WHAT YOU NEED
Tools: Spade; secateurs or pruning shears
Materials: Metal arches or similar support structure; plants; slow-release fertiliser; string

As a feature, a rose walkway will become even more attractive as it ages, especially if you choose rose cultivars selected for both colour and scent to adorn the sides and cover the top of the walkway. The scent is particularly important because much of the fragrance will be released between 1 and 3m (3 and 10ft) above the ground into the area where it can be fully appreciated by most people. Climbing roses such as *Rosa* 'Zepherine Drouhin' and *R.* 'Albertine' are ideal.

Consideration must also be given to the growth rate and habit of the plants to give even and balanced growth along the walkway. It is particularly important that the climbing roses be tied to the structure, not intertwined through it, because this makes maintenance of the structure much easier. It will then be possible to treat the structure with a preservative or carry out any repairs by removing the roses and repositioning them afterwards. Plant maintenance, such as pruning and training, is also much easier if the roses are not intertwined through the structure.

Tip: If you need to remove the roses to carry out maintenance work on the support structure of the walkway, it is best to do so at the same time of year as the roses are pruned in order to minimise disturbance to the plants.

Erect the supporting structure according to the manufacturer's instructions. Here, metal arches are installed along a pathway. Dig a hole large enough to accommodate the plant's root system 30–40cm (12–16in) away from the upright support.

Holding the plant by its woody stems, gently remove it from the container, teasing out any roots that are curling around the bottom of the root ball. Place the root ball in the hole and lean the top of the plant against the support.

Using a spade, pull the soil back into the hole around the plant's root ball and firm it gently into place. Sprinkle a liberal dressing of slow-release fertiliser onto the soil. This will be washed down into the root zone as the plant's roots start to spread out.

Spread out the strongest leading shoots against the support frame. Tie them into position so that they will start climbing in the right direction.

Continue to tie in any main shoots, and side shoots to fill any gaps between the main shoots. This will give an even spread of growth over the whole support frame.

As they develop, tie in new growths and cut out any surplus or badly damaged shoots. Reduce any thin shoots to about one-third of their original length. This will encourage them to produce more strong growths.

Flowering step lawn

Taking on a sloping garden can seem a daunting proposition, but rather than viewing the slope as a problem, try to see the design possibilities it offers. Aim to work with the slope rather than against it by trying to level it out, which could well involve a great deal of time, effort and expense. Creating a stepped lawn will transform the slope into an attractive and more functional feature and has the added advantage that fragrant plants can be incorporated into its design.

WHAT YOU NEED

Tools: String; wooden stakes; hammer; length of wood; spirit level; spade
Materials: Stones, bricks or similar material; fragrant plants such as *Dianthus* and *Thymus*

It is possible to cope with a sloping garden as long as a compromise can be reached over the work involved, such as having a lawn only where it is feasible to mow and trying to reduce the angle of the slope. Often by undertaking some minor adjustments to the levels, you can create a small terrace or series of terraces to make the slope into a feature. This could involve levelling some of the slope with soil held in place by a series of low retaining walls. The material used for these walls (such as stone or brick) can be chosen to blend in with the garden and its surroundings.

The height and distance between the steps will vary according to the angle of the slope. The steps will be much closer together on a steep slope and farther apart on a gentle slope. A stepped lawn can work perfectly on either a small or large scale, not only making maintenance easier but also providing the perfect setting for a range of low-growing fragrant plants without the need for separate borders.

> **Tip:** Use fragrant plants that prefer well-drained soil. *Dianthus*, for example, will thrive in planting pockets within a retaining wall because the wall provides good drainage.

Decide on the position of the steps according to the angle of the slope – a steep site will require more steps, closer together. Mark out the 'step lines' on the slope with string and stakes. The steps do not have to be placed at regular intervals if you want an informal design.

Check the levels to get some idea of how high the 'riser' (the front of the step) will be. Ideally, it should be no more than 30cm (12in) to make climbing easier. The size of the 'tread' (the part of the step you walk on) can be any convenient distance.

Dig a trench along the step line wide enough for the stones to fit into. Peel back the turf on the upper side of the slope by 30–60cm (1–2ft), depending on the angle of the slope.

Place the stones in position to form the riser of the step. Bed the stones into the bottom of the trench so that at least half of each stone is buried. Pack soil firmly into place around them.

Add more soil to raise the level of the soil behind the riser to about 5cm (2in) below the tops of the stones. Prepare the exposed soil behind the riser to a fine tilth and re-lay the turf, gently firming it into position.

Finish off the steps by planting a series of low-growing fragrant plants into the pockets between the stones.

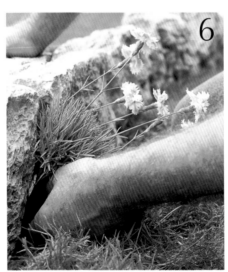

Container gardening

Patios, balconies and roof gardens are all places where hard surfaces dominate, leaving less scope for plants. The patio usually consists of an area set aside in a sunny spot, either next to the house or in another part of the garden, to provide a stable base for furniture for sitting and/or eating. Balconies and roof gardens may have more variable weather conditions because their situation is determined by the building rather than the direction of the sun. Whatever the location, you can make these areas as fragrant as the traditional garden by choosing appropriate plants for the wide range of attractive containers available.

Balconies and roof gardens

The main considerations for a balcony or roof garden are weight and stability, which may restrict the size of container, particularly if the site is exposed to regular strong wind. Precautions you can take include using containers with a wide, stable base, staking taller plants firmly when you plant them and keeping tall plants away from the edge. Another good idea is to fix trellis to the side walls to reduce the wind flow, with plastic mesh on the outside if necessary (it can be hidden behind plants on the inside).

Types of container

There is a vast choice of containers available to suit everyone's taste. Terracotta looks attractive and comes in natural, earthy colours, but check whether it is frost-proof or it may crack during the winter. Being porous, it allows the compost to lose moisture through the sides of the pot as well as from the surface, which can mean extra watering. Glazed pottery pots come in many colours and are ideal if you are designing around a colour theme and using matching paint on trellising or woodwork.

Plastic pots are lightweight, come in various colours and keep the compost moist because water is not lost through the sides. They may not look as natural as pottery containers but they can be disguised beneath the foliage or painted. They will last many years, although they may go brittle if they are in direct sunlight. Metal containers vary in weight and hold moisture well. However, they also conduct heat well and, if they are in direct sunlight, the roots inside can get very hot, resulting in damage.

Fragrant container plants

Most plants can be grown successfully in a container as long as they are looked after properly. Some of the best fragrant plants for growing in containers are:

- **Indoor fragrant plants**
  Freesia, Lilium, Hoya, Gardenia, Hyacinthus, Stephanotis, Citrus limon, Narcissus, Iris reticulata and *Jasminum*.

- **Outdoor fragrant plants**
  Abeliophyllum, Hamamelis, Laurus nobilis, Myrtus, Narcissus, Nicotiana, Sarcococca, Daphne, Lavandula and *Artemisia*.

This cast metal container has an intricate pattern of twining leaves that adds an extra decorative touch to a patio garden.

You do not have to restrict yourself to small plants in a container garden. Many smaller tree varieties will thrive in a container if well cared for.

Compost

The type of compost you use in your containers is more of a consideration on a balcony or roof garden than on a patio where weight does not matter.

Loamless composts

These are based on peat or coir rather than soil. Their advantages are that they weigh much less than loam-based compost and give good root aeration. However, they dry out quickly in hot weather, can be difficult to rewet and do not hold on to nutrients. They can also be unstable, especially when dry. Plants growing in this type of compost need watering and feeding more frequently.

Loam-based composts

These are heavy and therefore more stable than loamless composts. They also retain moisture and nutrients well. Loam-based composts are available in different strengths, so you can suit the compost to the plant being grown, from annual bedding to long-term fruit trees.

Growing plants in paving

You do not need a large garden to grow aromatic and fragrant plants. In fact, it is not necessary to have a garden at all, as many smaller plants can be grown in the cracks and crevices of walls or paving. These low-growing, ground-covering plants are ideal for softening the harsh outlines of an area of hard landscaping, such as a path or patio, which can look bare, especially when it is first laid.

WHAT YOU NEED
Tools: Small chisel; pointing trowel; brush; watering can or hose
Materials: Plants such as *Dianthus, Phlox, Viola odorata, Thymus* and *Chamaemelum*; compost

If you are laying a new path or patio, you can leave gaps in the paving where the plants can be positioned. In areas already surfaced, you will need to chip out some sand and mortar from the joints of the paving in order to create pockets for planting. How much sand and mortar is taken out will depend on the technique that was used to lay the paving and the type of base beneath, which must be broken through to allow adequate drainage for the plants. Soil may need to be dug out of the joint as well, but again, this depends on the method used when the paving was laid.

Encouraging plants to establish in pockets and allowing them to spread is also an attractive way of controlling weeds. The spreading plants will colonise the joints, depriving weed seeds of room to germinate and grow. Chamomile (*Chamaemelum nobile*) and thyme (*Thymus vulgaris*) will grow and spread quickly, and are resilient enough to tolerate being walked on now and again. Plants such as *Lavandula* x *intermedia* will provide fragrance and aroma, while *Oenothera triloba* produces a strong violet scent in the evening.

> **Tip:** Do not be tempted to use invasive plants, such as larger members of the mint family (*Mentha*), because they may undermine the paved area.

Using a small chisel, carefully chip out the mortar from the joint in the paving where the plant is to be positioned, taking great care to minimise disturbance to the surrounding hard surface.

With a pointing trowel, scrape out the sand and mortar from the opened joint in the paving. It is important to remove as much rubble as possible to create a pocket for the plant's roots to grow in.

Knock the plant from its pot and remove as much soil as possible, gently teasing out the roots. This makes the root ball as small as possible so that it can be lowered down into the planting pocket in the paving.

Using your fingers, gently insert the plant into the planting pocket. Press it into position and firm it into place. Let the plant sit slightly higher than the surface of the paving to allow for settling.

Use a brush to fill the rest of the planting pocket with compost. Tug the top of the plant gently a few times to coax more compost down around the roots of the plant.

Water the plant to help settle the compost around the roots. If all the compost washes down into the planting pocket, you may need to add more to the hole and water it in.

Citrus specimen plant

Citrus plants make ideal specimen plants for growing in the house or conservatory. Species such as *Citrus limon* have wonderful glossy leaves and attractive flowers that are pink in bud opening to pure white. The flowers are also highly fragrant and release a jonquil scent, so they are an excellent choice for filling a room with natural fragrance.

WHAT YOU NEED
Tools: Secateurs; water sprayer; soft cloth or tissue
Materials: Citrus plant; garden cane; string; washing detergent; leaf-shine solution; fertiliser

In mild climates, citrus plants can be given the protection of an indoor environment through the winter and then moved outdoors from late spring until early autumn. As with other plants, much of their growth is regulated by light level and temperature, but most citrus slip into dormancy when temperatures fall below 13°C (55°F). Species such as the *Citrus limon* used in this project will produce as many as five flushes of flowers each year, so it is not uncommon to see flower buds, flowers and fruit on the same plant at any given time.

Although citrus are both attractive and have very fragrant flowers, they do require care and attention to keep them growing well. The fact that they are constantly growing and have a natural tendency to form an open, straggly habit means that they need regular pruning and training if they are to form a strong branch structure that can cope with the weight of the fruits when they are produced.

> **Tip:** Great care must be taken if citrus trees are to be severely pruned because they have very limited food reserves in their woody tissue and removing a number of branches may lead to severe dieback of some of the remaining branches.

With new or young plants, start by tying the main central stem to a cane. Training the plant in this way helps to produce an upright stem on which a framework of branches can develop.

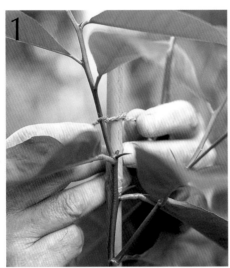

Snip out any shoots that may start to compete with the main stem and reduce side shoots by about one-third of their length to encourage them to become thicker and more sturdy.

It is important to do as much pruning as necessary while the shoots are young and soft. Older branches may die back after pruning and be prone to attack by fungal disease. These branches will need pruning a second time to remove the dead growth.

Where leaves have accumulated a layer of dirt, spray with lukewarm water containing a weak solution of detergent to soften the dirt. Several applications may be required.

Wipe the leaves with a soft cloth or tissue to clean the remaining dirt off the leaf surface. At this stage, a proprietary 'leaf-shine' solution can be applied to improve the leaf gloss if desired.

The plant will need a regular application of fertiliser and repotting because it is continuously growing, but only transfer it to a pot 2–3cm (1in) larger in diameter than the existing one. A move to a much larger pot would result in lots of stem growth and few flowers.

Planting a fragrant container

Growing fragrant plants in containers offers the opportunity to bring scent to even the smallest garden, to bring fragrance close to the house, seating areas and patios, and to cultivate the plants you want regardless of the soil in the rest of the garden. Some fragrant plants, such as sweet peas, roses, and jasmines, can also be grown 'vertically' allowing you to overcome space limitations by using features such as trellis, tripods and wigwams which support the plants without taking up much room in the garden.

WHAT YOU NEED

Materials: Large container; multi-purpose compost; sweet peas (*Lathyrus odoratus*); wigwam

Vertical gardening (growing upwards rather than sideways) using supports allows plants to develop fully without taking up much room either in the garden or on the patio in a container. Ideally, the structure should be chosen to suit the plant it will support. This is especially important for plants with twining stems or tendrils as there is a limit to the diameter of the support around which a plant can twine and grip – usually about the thickness of a pencil. Slender supports, such as thin wooden strips or bamboo canes, are ideal for plants such as sweet peas. They are strong enough to support the plants but thin enough to be obscured by foliage and flowers as the plants establish and cover the support.

A trellis wigwam covered in sweet peas makes a beautiful summer feature. Planting the peas inside the wigwam will cut down on maintenance time as you will not need to tie the plants into position or provide extra support. This is because the plants will naturally grow out into the light, growing past the support structure and gripping onto it as they grow. The climbers will also become self-supporting, clinging to each other as well as onto the structure where the supports are too thick.

> **Tip:** In the autumn, you can replant containers with fragrant bulbs, such as *Narcissus* 'Pheasant' Eye', to provide an excellent display of scent and colour the following spring.

Start by selecting a suitable container and filling it with compost to within 10cm (4in) of the rim (this should be the level after the compost has been gently firmed).

When the compost is up to the required level, remove the sweet peas from their pots and place them in the container, about 7–10cm (3–4in) inside the rim. Plant them into the compost and then firm them into position.

Position the base frame for the wigwam onto the rim of the pot and assemble it using small nuts and bolts. Leave the joints loose to allow for some adjustment when the wigwam is erected over the container.

Place the wigwam struts into their slots in the base frame and push them about 7–8cm (3in) into the compost to give the wigwam greater stability.

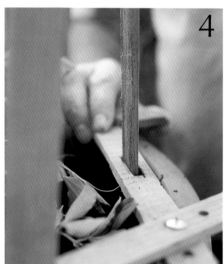

When all of the upright struts of the wigwam have been assembled and slotted into the base frame, gather them together at the top around a central finial and place a ring over the wigwam struts to hold them in position.

Planting the sweet peas inside the wigwam forces them to grow upwards and outwards, which means that their tendrils will cling to the wigwam as they grow through it.

Herbs for health

Throughout history, herbs have been used for medicinal purposes and to promote a feeling of well-being. Early monasteries and apothecary shops depended on having herb gardens to make potions. Some of the medicines in common use today have been synthesised from chemicals found in plants. If you enjoy cooking, you will also know that nothing beats the flavour of home-grown herbs. Keeping a range of different herbs in pots or a bed close to the kitchen or barbecue will allow you to pick them when they are needed to use fresh or to dry for later use.

Growing herbs

The herbs we grow at home originate from all over the world, so their growing requirements differ; most, however, prefer a sunny spot, with well-drained soil and shelter from cold winds. Some, such as basil (*Ocimum basilicum*), are only hardy in warm climates and need winter protection in colder areas. Others, like rosemary (*Rosmarinus officinalis*), are hardy in many regions, although they can still be affected by a cold snap.

Harvesting herbs

Once the plants are growing well, you can harvest them for drying as well as using them fresh. Some plants, like mint (*Mentha*), are so quick-growing that you may even find you are drying enough to supply friends and family as well as your own store cupboard. All you need is a warm, dark place to hang the stems as they dry and some airtight jars in which to store the crumbled leaves once they are ready (see pages 28–31 for more information on harvesting and drying).

Herbal teas

Many herbs can be used dried or fresh to make refreshing drinks that can be drunk hot or iced for pleasure or medicinal purposes. Chamomile (*Chamaemelum nobile*) is one of the most popular because it calms an upset stomach and anxious nerves as well as aiding a good night's sleep. Teas made from sage (*Salvia officinalis*) help concentration and are a good gargle for a sore throat.

To make a single infusion of chamomile or sage tea, use 5ml (1tsp) of the leaves of the herb to 250ml (1 cup) of water. Boil the water, wait 30 seconds, then sprinkle the leaves onto the water to steep, stirring periodically, for 10 minutes. Use a china or glass cup and pure water for the best results. Strain and drink it without milk, but sweeten with honey if you like.

Herb pillows

These date back to the days when sweet-smelling herbs were added to straw pillows in order to repel insects. Today, a small pillow or sachet is ideal for hanging near the bed at night to relax you. You can make a pillow to suit your individual needs, using a combination of leaves and flowers such as lavender (*Lavandula angustifolia*), mignonette (*Reseda odorata*), rosemary (*Rosmarinus officinalis*) and lemon verbena (*Aloysia triphylla*).

Jasmine flowers have an exquisite fragrance that can lift the spirits. This Jasminum x stephanense *is a hardy variety with pinkish flowers.*

Herbal baths

An aromatic herbal bath can be both pleasurable and therapeutic, especially after a busy day in the garden. Tie a large handful of leaves in a square of muslin cloth and hang it under the running water as the bath fills. To relax, try chamomile (*Chamaemelum nobile*), jasmine (*Jasminum officinale*), lime flowers (*Tilia*) or valerian (*Valeriana*). For stimulation, use basil (*Ocimum basilicum*), bay (*Laurus nobilis*), fennel (*Foeniculum vulgare*), lavender (*Lavandula angustifolia*), lemon balm (*Melissa officinalis*), lemon verbena (*Aloysia triphylla*), mint (*Mentha*), rosemary (*Rosmarinus officinalis*), sage (*Salvia officinalis*) or thyme (*Thymus vulgaris*). Healing herbs include marigold (*Calendula officinalis*), spearmint (*Mentha spicata*) and yarrow (*Achillea millefolium*).

*The fruit-scented creamy yellow flowers of the lime tree (*Tilia*) are perfect ingredients for a relaxing herbal bath.*

Herbal medicine

Many over-the-counter medicines are based on herbs. For example, in the past people used to chew a piece of willow bark to cure headaches. Investigation disclosed the presence of salicylic acid, which is now used to manufacture aspirin. Other herbal remedies include calendula ointment for cuts and grazes, arnica ointment for bruises and sprains and aloe vera gel for sunburn. Fresh from the garden, you can use plantain leaves (*Plantago*) on insect bites, feverfew leaves (*Tanacetum parthenium*) for migraine and mint (*Mentha*) for indigestion.

Companion planting

When plants are grown for their fragrance, the last thing you need is for the natural scent to be masked or retarded, which can happen when plants are sprayed with pesticides to control insect attack. One solution to this problem is to grow plants together as companions in order to reduce or even eliminate the need to spray. Scented plants are frequently used as companion plants to attract pests away from vegetables.

WHAT YOU NEED
Tools: Trowel, bulb planter or spade
Materials: Plants (see box below)

The chemical taint of pesticides can linger for days after spraying. It will have its own (usually unpleasant) smell and will certainly deter anyone from sampling the fragrance of even the most scented flowers. To make matters worse, some of these pesticides will kill or deter beneficial pollinating insects as well as the pest that has been targeted. Companion planting – where plants are grown together to protect one another from infestation by pest or attack by disease – is therefore a good solution. Companion plants work in two different ways: as host plants or as repellent plants. Host plants are attractive to certain pests and diseases and, because of that attraction, draw them away from the plants that require protection. Repellent plants work by driving pests and diseases away from certain areas or plants. In both cases, it is often the aroma or fragrance of these companion plants that has the desired effect.

Cultivated plants	Companion plants
Apple	Wallflower
Broad bean	Carrot, Celery
Cabbage	Beetroot, Chard
Lettuce	Carrot, Radish
Potato	Nasturtium, Tagetes
Raspberry	Marigold
Rose	Calendula, Chives, Garlic, Tagetes
Strawberry	Borage, Onion
Sunflower	Cucumber, Sweetcorn
Tomato	Basil, Carrot

Dig a hole large enough to accommodate the companion plant's root system. For smaller plants, a trowel or a bulb planter will be perfect for this. For larger plants, use a spade.

If the pot containing the companion plant is overcrowded, you can divide it into several clumps that can then be planted throughout the bed of cultivated plants. In this example, chives are being planted in a bed of roses.

Holding the plant by its root ball, place it in the hole with the base of the root ball on the floor of the hole.

Pull the soil back into the hole around the plant and firm gently into place. Make sure that the surface of the root ball is covered by soil. Water the plant to help settle the soil around the roots.

Wallflowers are often planted alongside members of the apple family to encourage pollinating insects. The insects are attracted to the early flowering wallflowers and then transfer to the apples when they come into flower.

Nasturtiums are often planted among potatoes to attract the aphid population to them and away from the potatoes. The nasturtiums are, in effect, used as 'sacrifice' plants to protect the potatoes, but their fragrance is a welcome bonus.

TREES

KEY INFORMATION

H: The average height the plant can reach

S: The average spread the plant can achieve

Sun/partial shade/shade: The position the plant prefers

Well-drained/moderate/moist/ water (for aquatics): How much water the plant needs

Acid/alkaline/neutral/any: The plant's preferred soil type

Z1 to Z10: The minimum winter temperature (zone) the plant can withstand

Zone 1: below –46°C (below –50°F)
Zone 2: –46 to –40°C (–50 to –40°F)
Zone 3: –40 to –34°C (–40 to –30°F)
Zone 4: –34 to –29°C (–30 to –20°F)
Zone 5: –29 to –23°C (–20 to –10°F)
Zone 6: –23 to –18°C (–10 to 0°F)
Zone 7: –18 to –12°C (0 to 10°F)
Zone 8: –12 to –7°C (10 to 20°F)
Zone 9: –7 to –1°C (20 to 30°F)
Zone 10: –1 to 4°C (30 to 40°F)

Drimys winteri
H 15m (46ft) S 10m (32ft)
Sun/partial shade
Well-drained
Any Z8

A native of South America, this relative of the magnolia is a vigorous tree with an upright habit and strongly aromatic ash-grey bark. The tough, leathery evergreen leaves are broadly lance-shaped, up to 20cm (8in) long, a dull dark green above and bluish-white beneath. From late spring into summer, creamy white flowers with a jasmine-like fragrance are produced in clusters of up to 20 blooms on the tips of the shoots. Propagate by sowing seed in a cold frame in autumn or taking semi-ripe tip cuttings in summer.

Hoheria glabrata
H 7m (23ft) S 7m (23ft)
Sun/partial shade
Well-drained/moderate
Alkaline/neutral Z8

This is a magnificent small tree from the south island of New Zealand. Its lax, flexible branches give it a broad, spreading, graceful habit. The deciduous glossy dark green leaves are up to 10cm (4in) long, broadly oval in shape but tapering to a point at the tip. In early to mid-summer, large numbers of fragrant, translucent white flowers up to 5cm (2in) across are produced in such profusion that they weigh down the branches. Propagate by sowing seed into pots and placing them in a cold frame in autumn or by taking semi-ripe cuttings in late summer or early autumn.

TREES

Magnolia x veitchii
H 25m (82ft) S 15m (46ft)
Sun/partial shade
Moderate
Acid/neutral Z6

This cultivated hybrid has some characteristics of both its parents, M. campbellii and M. denudata. It has an erect habit when young, changing to an open, spreading habit with age. The large, deciduous, spear-shaped leaves are tinted with purple when young, changing to mid-green with a paler coating on the underside as they mature. In early summer, it produces large, erect, goblet-shaped white flowers flushed with pink markings that are very sweetly scented. M. x veitchii 'Isca' has white flowers with pink markings at the base of each petal. Propagate by taking semi-ripe cuttings in late summer or layering in spring.

Robinia pseudoacacia 'Frisia'
H 10m (32ft) S 5m (16ft)
Sun
Moderate
Any Z5

The black locust or false acacia is a quick-growing tree that can sucker freely. Its young shoots have wine-red spines, and the bark of the trunk becomes deeply furrowed as the plant ages. The pinnate leaves change from golden yellow as they emerge to greenish-yellow in summer, then orange-yellow in autumn. Fragrant, white, pea-like flowers are produced in long, hanging clusters in summer, followed by brown seed pods. It can be pruned hard in early spring each year to control the size and produce larger leaves, or in summer (to avoid excessive bleeding) to maintain health. Propagate by grafting in winter.

Tilia x euchlora
H 20m (65ft) S 15m (46ft)
Sun/partial shade
Moderate
Alkaline/neutral Z4

This hybrid, deciduous lime makes an elegant tree when young, then develops a rounded, dense, straggly habit with low, hanging branches drooping almost to ground level as it ages. The broadly oval-shaped leaves have a finely toothed margin and are glossy, dark green on the upper surface and pale green on the underside. The sweetly scented yellowish-white flowers are borne in small clusters in mid-summer. This lime remains free of aphids, so there is no sticky 'honeydew', and the flowers often make honey bees drowsy. Propagate by budding and grafting or by layering in spring.

SHRUBS

Cytisus battandieri
H 3m (10ft) S 2m (7ft)
Sun
Moderate
Any Z7

The pineapple broom is a small
tree or large shrub, grown for its
pea-like, golden yellow, pineapple-
scented flowers that are carried in
tight clusters on the tips of branches.
The deciduous leaves are three-
lobed and covered with a layer
of fine silky hairs when young,
giving them an attractive silver
sheen that changes to a dull green
as they age. The dull-green stems
have a stiff, erect habit and often
turn a corky brown as they age.
Prune after flowering, although
note that this plant does not recover
from hard pruning into older wood.
Propagate by taking semi-ripe
cuttings in summer.

Genista aetnensis
H 8m (26ft) S 8m (26ft)
Sun
Well-drained/moderate
Any Z8

The Mount Etna broom is a large,
elegant, rounded deciduous shrub
with an upright habit and slender,
drooping, bright green branches that
are practically leafless. The tough,
sparse leaves are mid-green in
colour and strap-like, with fine
white silky hairs produced only
on the youngest shoots. Heavily
scented pea-like flowers are a
golden yellow colour and produced
in large quantities on the tips of
shoots in mid- and late summer.
If pruning this plant, do not cut
into old wood because it will
not regrow. Propagate by sowing
seed in spring.

Lavandula angustifolia
H 1m (3ft) S 1m (3ft)
Sun
Well-drained/moderate
Alkaline/neutral Z5

The English lavender has long,
narrow, aromatic silver-grey leaves
covered with fine, felt-like hairs that
are very effective for preventing
moisture loss. The small tube-like
flowers are carried in narrow
clusters (spikes) on tough square
stems. The form *L. a.* 'Hidcote' has
strongly scented, deep purple-blue
flowers and a compact, bushy habit.
There is a white-flowered form,
L. a. 'Alba', and the pink *L. a.*
'Rosea'. Propagate by taking semi-
ripe heel cuttings in late summer.

Philadelphus coronarius
H 3m (10ft) S 2.5m (8ft)
Sun/partial shade
Moderate
Any Z5

The mock orange is a deciduous
bushy shrub with a dense, upright
habit and thin, twiggy stems that
carry mid-green, oval leaves. In
summer, the dense spikes of small
creamy white flowers are noted for
their sweet, heady fragrance. There
are a number of cultivars with
attractively coloured leaves,
including *P. c.* 'Aureus' with pale
golden yellow leaves that turn
lemon green as they age, and *P. c.*
'Variegatus', which has mid-green
leaves decorated with an attractive
broad white margin. Propagate by
taking semi-ripe cuttings in summer
or hardwood cuttings in autumn.

Rosa rugosa
H 2.5m (8ft) S 4m (13ft)
Sun/partial shade
Moderate
Any Z2

This is a very tough, dense, vigorous
rose with a spreading, suckering
habit. The light grey-brown shoots
are densely covered with fine bristly
thorns (it is commonly called the
hedgehog rose) that carry leathery,
deeply veined, glossy, dark green
deciduous leaves that turn orange in
autumn. The large, single, deep-pink
flowers have an open cup shape
with a bright golden yellow centre,
and are followed in autumn by
large, round, bright red hips. The
cultivar 'Hansa' has very fragrant
semi-double scarlet flowers.
Propagate by taking semi-ripe
cuttings in summer or hardwood
cuttings in winter or spring.

Rosmarinus officinalis
H 1.5m (5ft) S 1.5m (5ft)
Sun
Well-drained/moderate
Any Z6

This is the popular cottage garden
rosemary that grows with a strong
spreading habit, developing into
an open-centred shrub with age.
The blue-green evergreen foliage is
strongly aromatic and very useful in
both cooking and herbal treatments.
Each leaf is narrow and leathery, a
suitable adaptation to resist moisture
loss in the hot Mediterranean
regions from which the species
originates. In late spring and early
summer, small, two-lipped, pale
lilac flowers are produced along
the stems, sometimes with a second
flush in autumn. Prune annually
after the first flowering, especially
if the foliage is to be harvested.
Propagate by taking semi-ripe
cuttings in summer.

CLIMBERS & WALL SHRUBS

Jasminum x stephanense

H 5m (16ft) S 3m (10ft)

Sun/partial shade

Well-drained

Any Z7

Found growing wild in south-west China, this hybrid of *J. beesianum* and *J. officinale* is a vigorous woody deciduous climber with a twining habit. The leaves are arranged in opposite pairs on green climbing stems. They are dull green in colour, broadly lance-shaped, up to 5cm (2in) long and arranged in groups of five along a central rib. The clusters of heavily fragrant pale pink flowers open to produce star-shaped blooms 2–3cm (1in) across. Prune after flowering by thinning out some of the older shoots. Propagate by taking semi-ripe cuttings in summer.

Lathyrus odoratus

H 2m (7ft) S 1m (3ft)

Sun

Well-drained

Any Z6

Originating from Italy, the annual sweet pea is a tall, vigorous, self-supporting climber with curling tendrils on the tip of each mid-green leaflet, with one pair of leaves. The flowers are heavily scented (especially in the evening) and come in a variety of colours, with pink, white and deep purple being the most popular. They are produced in clusters throughout the summer months. For vibrant colours and the most scented flowers, choose old-fashioned cultivars such as 'Cupani' and 'Painted Lady'. Propagate by sowing seed in autumn or spring and harden off before planting out in late spring or early summer.

Lonicera periclymenum

H 5m (16ft) S 5m (16ft)

Sun/partial shade

Moderate

Any Z4

The honeysuckle is a strong-growing, twining, woody climber, ideal for a wall, fence or pergola, with oval, mid-green deciduous leaves and heavily fragrant, tubular flowers. These are red and yellow-white, carried in clusters at the ends of the shoots and followed by poisonous red berries in autumn. In late spring to early summer, the form *L. p.* 'Belgica' has white flowers, flushed red-purple outside and fading to yellow, with a second display in late summer. *L. p.* 'Serotina' flowers mid-summer to mid-autumn; the flowers are rich red-purple outside and white inside fading to yellow. Prune to maintain shape by removing old wood after flowering. Propagate by taking hardwood cuttings in autumn.

CLIMBERS & WALL SHRUBS

Rosa 'Albertine'
H 15m (16ft) S 4m (13ft)
Sun
Moderate
Acid Z7

Raised in France in 1921, this
strong-growing deciduous rambling
rose is one of the most reliable ever
produced. It is ideal against a wall,
trellis or fence. The young growths
produce copper-brown leaves on
arching red-thorned, dull-red shoots.
The leaves turn a glossy mid-green
later. The richly fragrant salmon-pink
flowers, which become paler with
age, are fully double and about
7.5cm (3in) across. Pruning involves
cutting out the old flowered shoots
immediately after flowering and
removing any suckers that may
originate from the rootstock of a
grafted plant. These need to be
removed at their base or they
will dominate the top variety.
Propagate by taking hardwood
cuttings in late autumn.

Trachelospermum jasminoides
H 8m (26ft) S 8m (26ft)
Sun
Moderate
Any Z8

The star jasmine is a handsome
climbing plant with tough evergreen
leaves that are a glossy dark green
colour and arranged in opposite
pairs along thin, brown, twining
stems. The small jasmine-like
flowers are very fragrant, white with
a yellow eye in the centre and star-
shaped. They are borne in profusion
during early and mid-summer. The
cultivar *T. j.* 'Variegatum' has a
narrow white margin at the edge of
each leaf and also produces fragrant
flowers. Propagate by taking
softwood cuttings in summer or by
layering young shoots in autumn.

Wisteria floribunda
H 10m (32ft) S 10m (32ft)
Sun/partial shade
Moderate
Alkaline/neutral Z5

This is one of the most beautiful
of all climbing plants, particularly
when draped in cascades of
fragrant, pea-like flowers in early
summer as the leaves emerge.
The leaves are dark to mid-green
in colour and divided into small
leaflets. The plant grows best against
a sunny wall. It supports itself with
vigorous stems that twine in a
clockwise direction and grow up to
10m (32ft) in length. The vanilla-
scented flowers are white, reddish-
pink, blue or mauve. They open
from the base towards the tip and
fragrance can vary greatly between
cultivars. *W. f.* 'Multijuga' is very
fragrant. Propagate by layering,
grafting or taking softwood cuttings
in summer.

PERENNIALS & BULBS

Achillea millefolium
H 60cm (2ft) S 60cm (2ft)
Sun
Moderate
Any Z2

Commonly known as yarrow, this herbaceous perennial is an invasive, mat-forming plant with lance-shaped, finely divided, slightly hairy leaves of a dull mid-green colour. The finely cut foliage has a pungent aroma (feverfew) and is excellent for use in potpourris. The musk-scented flowers are held erect above the foliage in bold, flat clusters 7–10cm (3–4in) across from early until late summer, with colours ranging from deep reds through lilacs to pinks. One very popular form is *A. m.* 'Fanal', which has deep-red flowers, fading to orange as they age. Propagate by dividing in spring.

Artemisia 'Powis Castle'
H 60cm (2ft) S 1m (3ft)
Sun
Well-drained/moderate
Any Z8

This pretty woody-based perennial has highly aromatic silver foliage and is ideal for growing in a sunny border. The leaves are very finely divided, almost linear, and form a fluffy, rounded mound that ruffles with the slightest breeze and releases its fragrant oils if the foliage is touched. Small, silvery, yellow-tinted flowers are produced in clusters of up to 15cm (6in) long throughout late summer and autumn. This plant may be hard-pruned in spring to keep it compact. Propagate by taking soft-tip or heel cuttings in summer, especially in frost-prone areas where the plant may not survive the winter.

Dianthus chinensis
H 45cm (18in) S 30cm (12in)
Sun
Well-drained/moderate
Alkaline/neutral Z4

These plants form tufted mounds of silver-grey foliage, with thin leaves arranged in pairs on slender, silver-grey stems that are very narrow and spike-like. They are ideal for the front of a border or bed since they produce flushes of delicately scented, brightly coloured blooms on thin stems up to 45cm (18in) long, in colours ranging from white through many shades of pink to dark reds in summer and again in autumn. The cultivar 'Doris' has double blooms that are two-tone pink and heavily scented of cloves. Propagate by sowing seed in spring or taking cuttings of non-flowering shoots in summer.

Dianthus gratianopolitanus
H 20cm (8in) S 40cm (16in)
Sun
Moderate
Alkaline/neutral Z5

This pretty low-growing perennial
is known as the Cheddar pink and
grows to form a dense, spreading
mat of small, narrow, spiky-looking
grey-green leaves on woody-based
stems. From late spring into summer,
solitary flowers are produced on
short, wiry stems, just above the
height of the leaves. They are
strongly scented of cloves, with a
toothed edge to each petal, and
come in shades of pink, often with
a darker ring of colour in the centre.
Propagate by sowing seed or
dividing in spring.

Eryngium maritimum
H 40–100cm (16in–36in)
S 1.2m (4ft)
Sun Well-drained
Any Z5

This clump-forming herbaceous
perennial has tough, prickly leaves
that vary in colour from silver-grey
to grey-green, with the stems
showing the same variations in
colour. In late summer, tufted globes
of metallic silver-blue flowers, each
surrounded by a ruff of leathery
spines, are produced on the shoot
tips, the dead flowers often lasting
well into the winter. These plants are
unusual in that they have aromatic
roots, producing a strong scent of
parsnips when exposed. Propagate
by taking root cuttings or dividing
in spring. Some species are
cultivated by seed.

Hedychium coronarium
H 3m (10ft) S 1m (3ft)
Sun/partial shade
Moderate/moist
Any Z9

The white ginger lily is a herbaceous
perennial that originates from the
Indian subcontinent. It has a thick,
fleshy rootstock and a narrow,
upright habit, with long, pointed,
lance-shaped glossy green leaves
that often reach 45cm (18in) in
length. During late summer, very
fragrant butterfly-shaped flowers are
produced on spikes up to 20cm
(8in) long on stems often 2m (7ft)
tall. The flowers are white with
yellow markings at the base of each
petal. Propagate by sowing seed
into pots as soon as it is ripe and
placing the pots in a cold frame, or
by dividing the rhizomes in spring.

PERENNIALS & BULBS

Hemerocallis
H 1m (3ft) S 1m (3ft)
Sun/partial shade
Moderate
Any Z4

This colourful clump-forming plant has architectural, semi-evergreen, pale to mid-green, strap-shaped leaves, ending in a sharp point at the tip. The brightly coloured blooms only last for a single day in mid-summer but are produced in such rapid succession that this is hardly noticed. The lily-like flowers are produced in clusters on top of tall, erect stems. The species *H. lilioasphodelus* and its hybrids are particularly fragrant, with a scent similar to honeysuckle. *H. citrina* has very fragrant flowers that open in late afternoon and evening. Propagate by dividing in autumn.

Hosta
H 1m (3ft) S 60cm (2ft)
Partial shade
Moderate
Any Z6

This is one of the most beautiful herbaceous perennials, with small, trumpet-like pendulous flowers carried on tall green stems above the leaves from mid-summer. These plants are grown for their attractive foliage, and leaf shapes range from long and narrow through to oval with a pointed tip. Colours vary from blue through to rich combinations of silver or golden variegations. The form 'Honeybells' has fragrant white flowers, sometimes striped blue, and 'Invincible' has fragrant pale mauve flowers. Propagate by dividing in early spring.

Lilium
H 1.2m (4ft) S 25cm (10in)
Sun/partial shade
Moderate
Any Z6

These glorious plants have bold, trumpet-like blooms made up of six petals that curl open to develop into an open star shape that can vary in size from 2.5cm (1in) to 25cm (10in) across, depending on the variety. They are among the most highly scented flowers available. The leaves are pale to dark green, some are narrow, almost grass-like, and grouped at the base of the plant, while others produce leaves in clusters (whorls) at intervals along the stems that often reach 1m (3ft) tall, topped by flowers in late summer or early autumn. Propagate from scales in autumn.

PERENNIALS & BULBS

Salvia
H 30–150cm (12–60in)
S 23–60cm (9–24in)
Sun Well-drained/moderate
Any Z9

Salvia is a large genus of annuals, biennials, perennials and shrubs, distinguished by their colourful two-lipped flowers in summer. Many have aromatic foliage, including *S. officinalis* (sage), which is used in cooking. The annual *S. viridis* 'Claryssa' is dwarf and bushy, with brightly coloured bracts of purple, pink or white. Bedding forms include *S. splendens* 'Blaze of Fire' and 'Red Arrows', both with bright red flowers. Blue-flowered forms include *S. patens*, a tuberous perennial with hairy leaves, and *S. guaranitica*, a sub-shrub with long, deep-blue flowers. Propagate annuals and perennials by sowing seed in spring, and in summer for biennials. Take semi-ripe cuttings of shrubs in late summer.

Thymus
H 30cm (12in) S 30cm (12in)
Sun
Well-drained/moderate
Any Z5

This genus includes around 350 species of low-growing, hardy, evergreen herbaceous perennials and sub-shrubs with aromatic leaves. Some are mat-forming and prostrate; others form small shrubs with thin, twiggy stems. The small leaves are usually oval and grey-green, sometimes hairy. Mat-forming types form dense carpets. *Thymus* x *citriodorus* is a small shrubby plant with lemon-scented leaves up to 1cm (½in) long, and tiny pale lilac flowers in clusters on the tips of the branches during summer. *T.* x *c.* 'Aureus' has golden leaves tinged with green, and *T.* x *c.* 'Silver Queen' has silver and green variegated leaves. Propagate by taking semi-ripe cuttings in summer.

Viola tricolor
H 13cm (5in) S 15cm (6in)
Sun/partial shade
Moderate
Any Z4

The heartsease or wild pansy is a small tuft-forming annual, biennial or short-lived perennial ideal for a border or container. It has toothed heart-shaped leaves and pretty, delicately scented three-coloured flowers during spring, summer and into autumn. Of the five petals, the upper two are dark purple or violet, the central two paler purple and the bottom one yellow streaked with violet. The colours are not definite, and the middle petals may be almost white or as dark as purple. The form 'Bowles' Black' is very deep violet with a yellow eye. This plant is short-lived (from seed sown in spring) but sets seed easily and may be invasive.

ANNUALS & BIENNIALS

Calendula officinalis 'Fiesta Gitana'
H 30cm (12in) S 30cm (12in)
Sun/partial shade
Well-drained/moderate
Any Z8

This marigold is a compact, fast-growing annual plant with multiple stems and lance-like, hairy, aromatic foliage. Throughout summer and autumn, it produces daisy-like double flowers in shades of orange and yellow with darker orange centres. Use this plant for an added splash of colour at the front of a border, or in a container or window box. Regular dead-heading will prevent it from setting seed and will ensure a continuous succession of flowers. Any seed that does form and is shed is likely to grow the following year. Propagate by sowing seed in the final growing position in late spring.

Datura inoxia
H 1m (3ft) S 1.2m (4ft)
Sun
Moderate
Any Z9

Commonly called the Indian apple, this half-hardy annual originates from central South America. It is grown for its exceptional display of 30cm (12in) white, heavily scented, trumpet-shaped flowers. These pendulous flowers are produced singly or in groups of three during the summer months and open in the evening. The large evergreen leaves, up to 25–30cm (10–12in) in length, are oblong with an elongated point. They are a mid-green colour with wavy margins and are covered with a coating of soft, felt-like hairs. Propagate by taking semi-ripe heel cuttings under protection in early summer.

Heliotropium arborescens
H 45cm (18in) S 40cm (16in)
Sun
Moderate
Any Z10

This tender evergreen shrub is usually grown as an annual for display purposes. The thick, textured, wrinkled leaves are dark green in colour and oblong in shape. They are carried on dark green, almost black, stems. The small flowers are formed in 10cm (4in) flat clusters and are very fragrant, with colours varying from a deep bluish-purple through to lavender and pure white. Some types can be raised from seed, including the newer 'Mini Marine' with its compact, bushy habit, bronze-green leaves and violet-purple flowers. Propagate by taking cuttings in autumn or sowing seed in spring.

ANNUALS & BIENNIALS

Limnanthes douglasii
H 15cm (6in) S 25cm (10in)
Sun
Moderate
Any Z8

This hardy annual is a low-growing
plant with thin, creeping stems
covered in bright green leaves with
a lightly toothed margin. It spreads
by self-seeding. It is grown for its
sweetly scented, saucer-shaped
flowers, which have yellow centres
and a white margin to each petal,
giving it the common name of
poached-egg plant. It is ideal for
attracting beneficial insects into
the garden because, in addition
to its scent, it also produces nectar
to attract bees and butterflies. In
mild, sheltered places this plant
can survive outdoors over winter.
Propagate by sowing seed in
early to late spring.

Lobularia maritima
H 15cm (6in) S 23cm (9in)
Sun
Moderate
Any Z7

This member of the cabbage family
originates from the Canary Islands.
It is a low-growing annual with a
spreading, branching habit and
slightly hairy, grey-green leaves
that are narrow, strap-like and up
to 2–3cm (1in) long. Throughout
summer, tiny, cross-shaped, sweetly
fragrant flowers are produced in
clusters often reaching 7–8cm (3in)
across. These blooms are usually
pure white or occasionally pinkish-
white or purple. Dead-heading
the flowers will encourage the
production of a second display
of flowers later. Propagate by
sowing seed in the final growing
position in late spring.

Lupinus luteus
H 75cm (30in) S 30cm (12in)
Sun
Moderate
Acid/neutral Z6

This striking annual plant has mid-
green stems, thickly covered with
soft, slender hairs. The pale to
mid-green, broadly oval leaves
are narrower towards the base
and sparsely covered in a coating
of fine, soft, shaggy hair. In mid-
summer, bright yellow flowers with
the scent of vanilla are arranged in
a circle or whorl at the end of the
stem. In the autumn, these are
followed by small, black, hairy
pods, each containing an average
of five slightly flattened black seeds.
Propagate by sowing seed in the
final growing position in spring; pre-
soak the seed in water for 24 hours.

ANNUALS & BIENNIALS

Matthiola incana

H 15–75cm (6–30in)
S 23–30cm (9–12in)
Sun Moderate
Alkaline/neutral Z6

There are various forms of stock, most of which are grown as annuals, although some are perennial if they are left to grow. They have grey-green leaves and flower profusely through the summer in upright spikes of fragrant purple, violet, mauve, pink or white double or single blooms. There are many seed mixes, in various heights and multiple colours, including 'Cinderella' (spicy, clove scent, double, dwarf), 'Legacy' (long flowering season, double, strongly fragrant) and 'Ten Week Mixed' (compact, highly fragrant, quick-growing annual). Propagate by sowing seed in summer for the longest flowering season the following year, overwintering under cover to prevent fungal attack.

Mirabilis jalapa

H 1m (3ft) S 1m (3ft)
Sun
Well-drained
Any Z8

This is a bushy tender perennial plant (often grown as an annual), with broadly oval, mid-green leaves arranged in opposite pairs on fleshy green stems, often with dark red or purple markings around the leaf joints. The large trumpet-shaped flowers are white, yellow, red or magenta and open in the afternoon, hence the common name of four o'clock flower. They are heavily fragrant and are at their most scented in the evening. They die by morning to be replaced by more flowers the following afternoon. Propagate by sowing seed outdoors in late spring or dividing in spring.

Nicotiana x sanderae

H 25–60cm (10–24in)
S 30–45cm (12–18in)
Sun Moderate
Any Z7

This ornamental relative of tobacco is a multi-branched and stout-stemmed plant that grows as an annual, biennial or sometimes short-lived perennial, according to the conditions. The wavy-edged leaves grow as a basal rosette, from which the tall flowering stem rises. The individual flowers have a tube up to 9cm (3½in) long, flaring into a wide trumpet shape with five rounded lobes. They are available in white and shades of red, pink, purple and even lime-green and release their scent in the evening. Propagate by sowing seed in spring as summer bedding in a border or in a container. Compact forms, such as 'Domino Mixed', are ideal for a container.

ANNUALS & BIENNIALS

Pelargonium
H 15–60cm (6–24in)
S 15–60cm (6–24in)
Sun/partial shade
Well-drained/moderate   Any Z10

Pelargoniums are grown for their bright, attractive flowers and/or their scented foliage. Regal cultivars are evergreen perennials with thick, branching stems, hairy, toothed, palm-like leaves and large, showy flowers in white, pink, salmon, orange, red or purple. Scented-leaf forms have smaller flowers and finely cut, toothed or finely lobed foliage with fragrances such as lemon, peppermint, orange, lime or balm. Zonal pelargoniums have smooth, succulent stems and large, rounded leaves. The flowers may be single, semi-double or double in white, orange, pink, red, purple and yellow. Trailing forms have ivy-like foliage and single or double flowers in white, purple, red, pink and mauve. Propagate by taking tip cuttings from non-flowering shoots in early or late summer.

Petunia
H 30cm (12in)
S 30–90cm (12–36in)
Sun Moderate
Any Z7

Although many petunias are herbaceous perennials, they are treated as half-hardy annuals that flower in the first season from seed, and are one of the most popular plants for hanging baskets, tubs and window boxes. They are colourful plants and come in white and shades of cream, pink, red, mauve, blue and a variety of striped forms, most with a vanilla fragrance, especially at night. The leaves, carried on green, hairy stems, are broadly oval, mid- to dark green in colour and sticky to touch. Dead-head the flowers regularly to keep the plants continually flowering. Propagate by sowing seed in spring.

Phacelia tanacetifolia
H 1.2m (4ft) S 45cm (18in)
Sun
Well-drained
Any Z10

This is a hardy annual originating from the south-western United States and Mexico. The mid-green leaves are about 25cm (10in) long but are divided into large numbers of smaller sub-divided leaflets that are broadly lance-shaped. The entire surface of the plant is covered with a layer of short hairs and contact with the skin may aggravate skin allergies. The blue or lavender-blue bell-shaped flowers are held above the leaves in dense, curved clusters and emit a strong heliotrope fragrance from mid-summer through into autumn. Propagate by sowing seed in the final growing position in early spring or autumn.

ANNUALS & BIENNIALS

Phlox drummondii
H 10–60cm (4–24in) S 30cm (12in)
Sun
Moderate
Any Z6

The half-hardy annual phlox is
grown for its attractive, brightly
coloured, fragrant flowers. They
may be single or double, in white
or shades of purple, red, pink or
lilac, and are carried in dense
clusters up to 7.5cm (3in) across on
the tips of the shoots from mid- to
late summer. It has an upright habit
and narrow, strap-like leaves of
mid- to light green, carried in pairs
on slender green stems. Available
forms include named cultivars such
as 'Double Chanel' (rich pale pink,
double) and mixed-colour seed
collections such as 'Tapestry' (rich
violet, yellow, salmon, pink and
red). Dead-head regularly for
continuous flowering. Propagate
by sowing seed in spring.

Tropaeolum majus
H 1.5m (5ft) S 1.5m (5ft)
Sun
Moderate
Any Z8

This is a climbing or trailing hardy
annual with rounded, light green
leaves, sometimes marked with
white splashes. The long-spurred,
broadly trumpet-shaped flowers are
about 5cm (2in) across and borne
throughout summer and autumn in
shades of yellow, cream, orange and
red, often with a contrasting splash
in the throat. The scented flowers
are edible and look colourful in a
salad. There are many seed mixes
available, including 'Trailing Mixed',
'Out of Africa' (white-marbled
leaves) and 'Gleam Mixed' (less
vigorous, to 38cm/15in). Grow
in containers, hanging baskets or
at the front of a border. Propagate
by sowing seed in spring (indoors,
or outdoors once the risk of frost
has passed).

Verbena bonariensis
H 2m (36in) S 45cm (18in)
Sun
Moderate
Any Z9

Usually grown as an annual, this
verbena will overwinter in milder
areas or in a frost-free greenhouse to
form a clump-forming perennial.
The tall, branching, wiry stems bear
a few oblong to lance-shaped leaves
and are topped by flattened clusters
of tiny lilac-purple flowers from
mid-summer to early autumn. The
flowers have a delicate fragrance
and are particularly attractive to
butterflies. Deadhead in late
summer to extend flowering. It will
self-seed or can be propagated by
sowing seed in autumn or spring
(sow under cover in cold areas), or
by dividing in spring.

AQUATICS & MARGINALS

Aponogeton distachyos
H 10–15cm (4–6in) S. 1.2m (4ft)
Sun/partial shade
Water
Z9

The water hawthorn is a moderately
vigorous aquatic perennial that, in
most winters, remains evergreen.
Its mid-green oblong-shaped leaves
have maroon markings and float on
the water surface from a submerged
rhizome. Clusters of small
hawthorn-scented flowers are
carried on forked branches just
above the water from spring right
through to autumn. Each small
white blossom has purple-black
stamens at its base and is wrapped
by a white spathe. Grow in soil
or planting baskets at the bottom
of water 30–90cm (12–36in)
deep. As the rhizome is almost
impossible to divide, propagate
by dividing clumps during the
growing season, or sowing seed
as soon as it is ready.

Iris pseudacorus
H 1m (3ft) S 25cm (10in)
Sun/partial shade
Moist
Any Z5

Commonly called the yellow flag,
this is a vigorous and extremely
hardy true water iris (although it
will grow in a border). It is easy
to grow, often forming large clumps
of tall, deciduous, blue-green,
strap-like leaves with pronounced
ribs running the full length of each
leaf. Tall, erect, green branching
stems carry at least five bright
yellow, scented blossoms with
small black or chocolate brown
markings during summer. The form
I. p. 'Variegata' has yellow stripes
running along the foliage. Propagate
by sowing seed in spring and early
summer, or by dividing immediately
after flowering.

Nymphaea
H 5cm (2in)
S 40cm–3m (16in–10ft)
Sun Water
Z3–10

The waterlily is the queen of
aquatic plants and ranges in size
from small to enormous. Small
varieties will fit in a half-barrel or
waterproof container; large ones
need a pond. These deciduous
herbaceous perennials produce
dark green or bronze-tinted circular
floating leaves, followed by open,
star-like, sometimes scented flowers
in colours from white to shades of
yellow, pink, orange and red. The
flowers and leaves rise from a thick
rootstock anchored securely in the
soil base or in a planting basket.
Fragrant forms include 'Caroliniana
Rosea' (soft-pink flowers), 'Marliacea
Albida' (white, flushed pink outside)
and *N. odorata* types. Propagate
by lifting and dividing the rootstocks
in spring.

chapter five

5

Plants for autumn

There are some plants that only really come into their own in the autumn, such as the fern-leaf clematis (*Clematis cirrhosa*), which will actually start to flower as the days shorten. A number of herbaceous plants also provide their best display of fragrance and colour at this time of year. Other plants will only consider flowering once they have shed their leaves, and some evergreens begin to produce deeply fragrant flowers that are barely visible under the canopy of thick, leathery leaves. Autumn is also a good time for displays of bulbs, even though they are a group of plants more commonly associated with spring. Carpets of scented blooms look spectacular, especially under trees or in partially shaded areas where the fragrance lingers.

Trees

One notable plant for this time of year is the deciduous tree *Cercidiphyllum japonicum*, whose leaves provide outstanding autumn colours, with tints of orange, red and even pink before turning butter yellow. The real bonus with this tree is that, as the leaves change colour, they release the aroma of hot sugar, resulting in the common name of candyfloss tree. Other trees, such as *Prunus subhirtella* 'Autumnalis Rosea', will start to flower soon after leaf-fall, producing clouds of tiny almond-scented blossoms throughout the autumn, winter and early spring.

When leaf-fall begins, it also allows more light into the shaded areas under the trees, encouraging plants such as *Cyclamen* to emerge and flower. Any plantings beneath trees often have their highest light levels at this time of year, having been dormant through the summer when the soil was dry and shaded.

Climbers and wall shrubs

There are several interesting fragrant climbers that flower at this time. The sweetly scented *Clematis rehderiana* flowers in early autumn, followed by the later flowering *Clematis flammula*, with its hint of hawthorn fragrance. *Lonicera japonica* has lemon-scented flowers until mid-autumn, often later in a mild year, and *Jasminum officinale* will still produce sweetly scented white flowers until the frosts stop it.

Wall shrubs for autumn include *Ceanothus* 'Gloire de Versailles', with its pale blue flowers giving a sweet scent that will waft in through an open window on a warm day. The season can last slightly longer with these plants because some extra warmth is provided by the residual heat from the wall or fence.

Shrubs

Some of the fragrant plants that flower in the autumn have an air of mystery about them. *Elaeagnus* x *ebbingei* has small, heavily fragrant flowers that are so well hidden by the tough, leathery leaves that it is the nose rather than the eye that leads you to the flower. Other deciduous shrubs with fragrant flowers that carry on into the autumn include *Buddleja davidii*, with its minute tubular flowers whose fragrance acts like a magnet to butterflies. Its close relative *Buddleja fallowiana* will also still be flowering into the first half of autumn.

The pretty white and yellow flowers of Romneya coulteri *will bloom in autumn and fragrance the air with their sweet scent.*

Bulbs and corms

Many bulbs and corms flower at this time of year. They have lain dormant during the warmer months but start to emerge in early autumn and produce flowers. *Cyclamen hederifolium* and *Crocus sativus* carry a mild scent and are best mass-planted in order to appreciate their fragrance because they are so low-growing. Some of the most strongly scented lilies continue to flower into the autumn, including *Lilium auratum, L. henryi* and *L. speciosum*, whose heady scent you can usually smell long before they come into view. These can therefore be planted more sparsely while still producing plenty of fragrance in the garden.

Annuals and biennials

Although most plants will be coming to the end of their life cycle, some will continue to produce flowers right up until the first frosts. Evening scents can be prominent at this time of the year, with *Oenothera biennis* and *Nicotiana sylvestris* producing their rich, sweet fragrance as the temperature falls and the daylight fades, drawing moths for pollination.

Perennials

A large number of perennials naturally flower in the second half of the year, providing colour and scent into the autumn. Plants such as *Gladiolus callianthus* 'Murieliae' and *Romneya coulteri*, both with white, sweetly scented flowers, and a number of different types of *Phlox* also flower in autumn, with *P. maculata* and *P. paniculata* producing flowers that are both attractive and fragrant.

Many herbaceous perennial plants that are left in position all year round will continue flowering well into the autumn, stopping only when the first hard frosts turn the foliage black, marking the end of another year of growth and causing the plants to die back down to ground level.

Autumn weather and its effects

The weather can be erratic in the autumn, with warm, sunny days, cool nights and damp humidity, as well as wind and rain. The only constant is that the days are getting shorter, a fact that is responsible for major changes within the plants, both visible and unseen. Some of these changes will result in leaf-fall in deciduous plants, and a toughening of the cells to help them cope with the cold weather of the oncoming winter. The changes can be deceptive, for although many plants appear to be approaching dormancy, they do not actually rest completely until well into the depths of winter.

Jobs for autumn

As the heat of summer begins to wane, autumn is a time of mellow days and golden light. Much of the autumn is spent tidying the garden as plant growth gradually slows down, but many of the tasks carried out now not only clear away the evidence of one growing season but are equally important in preparing the garden for the next. Autumn is a time of balance between the summer past and the winter ahead, so it is the ideal season to make plans for the following year's garden. Learn from this year's successes and failures, and use the lessons to plan future gardening projects. If you are keen to experiment, collect seed catalogues and select some new cultivars of seeds or plants to try out. This will create added interest as well as introduce new fragrances into areas of the garden or indoors.

Mulching

Applying a mulch to the soil in autumn can benefit plants considerably, especially if the mulch is an organic one. The soil is still warm from the summer, so applying a covering now will keep this residual heat trapped in the soil for a longer period. Although this will not extend the growing period of the plants, their root development can continue for several more weeks so that they gain a slightly earlier start the following spring. If the mulch is applied just after leaf-fall and all of the fallen leaves are cleared away beforehand, the spores of fungal diseases such as rose black spot that overwinter on the soil are suppressed.

Insulating containers

Plants growing in containers will need some protection over the coming months because the roots are the part most vulnerable to frost damage. Some form of insulation material, such as bubble plastic or horticultural fleece, would certainly improve the plants' chance of survival. Wrap the material loosely around the containers (not the plants) so that a layer of air between the container and the wrapping provides additional insulation.

Support structures

Many plants, especially those with long trailing growths, are susceptible to physical damage as the weather becomes more unsettled and the winds become stronger. Climbers and wall shrubs suffer more damage from poor or inadequate tying and support than any form of pest or disease, and most of the injury occurs in autumn and winter. During early to mid-autumn, tie in any new shoots that are to be kept and check the ties on old established growths to make sure they are not cutting into stems and branches. Replace any worn ties and strings. If the support structure for these plants is damaged, tie the long straggly growths of the plants into loose bunches and, after leaf-fall, replace or repair the supports before spreading the growths out and tying them into position.

Any young trees that have stakes and ties should be checked to make sure that the stake is in a sound, firm condition to keep the root system stable in windy conditions. Tree ties should be examined to make sure they are not frayed or worn and that they are not constricting the stem of the tree in any way.

The Mexican orange blossom (Choisya ternata) produces musk-scented flowers from late summer to autumn. Remove the dead flower heads in late autumn to ensure another good display the following spring.

Autumn is the time to harvest seeds from flowers such as the tobacco plant (Nicotiana alata).

Dead-heading

As plants gradually finish flowering, remove the dead flower heads. Some can be saved and used in potpourri (see page 30), such as the old flowers of the bergamot (*Monarda didyma*). Dead-heading in early autumn will encourage plants to produce a few more late flowers or hang on to their flowers slightly longer, whereas dead-heading in late autumn will keep the plants tidy and reduce the amount of damage done to the base of the plant as the stems rock in the winter winds.

Harvesting

This time of year is always associated with harvesting (see pages 28–31). Many plants, such as *Amberboa mochata* and *Nicotiana alata*, will have produced seeds that need to be harvested to form the basis of the following year's design. Mark the best plants when they flower to be sure only their seed is saved. Wait until the seed heads are just about to split before harvesting them and laying them in trays or on sheets of paper in a dry, cool room to allow the seeds to emerge naturally. All collected seed should be stored in labelled airtight containers in a cool, dark place. Replace harvested plants with some that will provide displays of colour and fragrance during late winter and early spring.

Propagation & planting

Many late summer-flowering plants will continue to provide colour and fragrance well into the autumn mists as the flowers make one last effort to produce seed. The leaves may be colourful and the air sweet with the scent of ripe fruit, but far from a state of happy complacency, you should be preparing for the following year to ensure that everything is ready for another glorious display once the colder months are over. This is the time of year to take out winter insurance, propagating any plants that are marginally hardy and may succumb to a very cold or very wet winter, giving you back-up for the following spring if required. The soil is still warm in autumn, so it is also an ideal time for introducing some new plants into the garden. These will be in good condition to get off to a quick start the following spring as the soil begins to warm up again.

Seedlings

Sweet peas (*Lathyrus odoratus*) can be sown in pots of loam-based compost in autumn and grown in a cold frame over winter. These can be transplanted outdoors during late spring the following year. For maximum scent, choose old-fashioned cultivars such as 'Cupani' and 'Painted Lady'. This is also a good time of year to collect and sow the seeds of woody plants. This should be done just before the seeds and fruits are fully ripe. Plants such as roses (*Rosa*) produce their seeds inside a fleshy hip or berry-like fruit. Separate the seed from this outer coating before sowing. Other plants, such as Japanese maple (*Acer japonicum* and *A. palmatum*), produce dry fruits that can be sown in the garden directly after collection.

Cuttings

Marginally hardy and some hardy plants can be propagated from semi-ripe cuttings in the autumn before the frosts. Alternatively, many trees and shrubs can be propagated at this time of year from hardwood cuttings.

Semi-ripe cuttings

Take semi-ripe cuttings (an intermediate growth stage between softwood and hardwood) from the tips of marginally hardy plants such as sage (*Salvia officinalis*), French lavender (*Lavandula stoechas*) and *Penstemon*. Grow them in a cold frame or unheated greenhouse until they have rooted, and root them in a slightly dry atmosphere to ensure that they do not rot. Many aromatic plants that have silver leaves hail from Mediterranean regions and succumb to the combination of cold and wet conditions rather than just low temperatures. Hardy plants such as *Mahonia*, *Osmanthus* and *Skimmia* can also be propagated from semi-ripe cuttings, but they need a more humid environment to keep them alive until they form roots.

Hardwood cuttings

Trees and shrubs such as the mock orange (*Philadelphus*), buffalo currant (*Ribes odoratum*) and *Viburnum farreri* will all root from hardwood cuttings taken from the current season's growth. These plants can be rooted out in the garden and will need no protection over the winter. Even though no leaves will develop until spring, they will often form new roots by mid-winter and will be suitable for planting out within a year.

*Take hardwood cuttings from shrubs such as the mock orange (*Philadelphus*) during autumn. They can be planted out within a year.*

Bulbs

Early autumn is also the ideal time for planting many of the spring-flowering bulbs. In the warm, moist soil, they will start to produce roots within a few weeks of planting even though it may be several months before any leaves become visible above ground. Scented *Narcissus* such as 'Bunting', 'Cheerfulness', 'Quail', 'Old Pheasant's Eye' and 'Queen Anne's Jonquil' are ideal for naturalising and provide plenty of fragrance through until early May.

Fragrant bulbs that are to be used for indoor displays, such as tulips (*Tulipa*) and hyacinths (*Hyacinthus*), can be potted now and prepared for 'forcing' (see pages 62–63), ready to provide scent and colour from mid-winter through to early spring. Lily-of-the-valley (*Convallaria majalis*) can be induced to flower by mid-winter and varieties of *Narcissus*, which hardly need any forcing at all, can be potted up in the autumn to be in flower throughout late winter and early spring.

Trees and shrubs

Autumn is an excellent time for planting shrubs, conifers and trees while the soil is still warm. The roots will have several weeks to begin to establish, even after the top of the plant has become dormant. This will not only help it survive the winter but will also give it a head start in spring because it will be ready to grow as soon as the temperatures begin to rise. Trees that are planted now should be firmly staked because the windiest time of the year is approaching. Climbers and wall shrubs should be either tied to a support system or pruned back to prevent any loosening of the roots or damage to branches and stems as a result of 'windrock'.

This is a good time of year to plant conifers or broad-leaved evergreens because they go through a burst of growth in early autumn. However, they must have some protection from strong winds that may draw moisture from the foliage before the new roots have established, which in turn could cause desiccation of the leaves, making them turn brown.

Autumn is also an ideal time to plant hedge shrubs (see pages 144–145) that will act as windbreaks to protect the more vulnerable plants in the garden from wind damage. The hedge will filter the wind and cause less turbulence than a solid barrier, such as a wall. Mixed-variety – or 'tapestry' – hedges look wonderful and can be a source of colour and fragrance through the changing seasons.

Mediterranean border

Many fragrant plants originate from countries where temperatures are quite hot at certain times of the year. In fact, some plants with aromatic foliage, such as lavender (*Lavandula*) and *Nepeta*, even produce stronger scent as temperatures rise. These plants lend themselves to cultivation on a hot, sunny site, especially where the soil is light, sandy and particularly free-draining. A striking Mediterranean-style border can be created by growing a selection of plants with contrasting aromatic leaves.

WHAT YOU NEED
Tools: Spade; knife; trowel; wheelbarrow; garden fork
Materials: Plastic membrane; container-grown plants such as *Artemisia, Cistus ladanifer, Cordyline australis, Lavandula angustifolia,* or *Santolina chamaecyparissus*; pebble/slate mulch

In a warm, sunny site, it makes sense to use some form of mulch over the border soil to help suppress weed growth (by preventing light from reaching the soil) and the amount of water being lost from the soil due to evaporation. Materials such as gravel, shingle and different grades of pebbles have become very popular as a means of covering the soil and reducing garden maintenance. Grey or blue slate chippings can also be used as an alternative to pebbles, providing an attractive contrast to the plants' foliage. Cover the soil with a water-permeable sheet or membrane, such as woven black plastic, before the stones are laid to reduce the quantity of stones required, to provide an adequate covering to control weeds and to limit evaporation.

The plants selected for this style of border must be carefully chosen to cope with particularly warm, dry conditions (the heat reflected from the stones will also increase temperatures by creating a very hot microclimate). The best plants to choose are therefore those with leaves adapted to cope with bright sunny conditions. This includes plants with silver or grey foliage, a covering of felt or hairs over the leaf surface, or long, strap-like leaves.

> **Tip:** To avoid swamping smaller plants, cover them with an upturned plant pot before spreading the mulching material, then remove the pot – this is easier than having to pick gravel or chippings out of the plants' foliage.

Start by clearing and levelling the area before planting begins. Place a sheet of heavy-gauge woven black plastic over the bed and seal the edges by tucking them in at least 15cm (6in) deep, stretching the plastic as tight as possible.

Using the heel of your boot or shoe, firmly close the groove in the soil that is holding the plastic sheeting.

Using a sharp knife, cut a cross in the plastic at the point where each plant is to be placed, and fold back the flaps of plastic to reveal the soil beneath.

Use a trowel to dig out a planting hole large enough to accommodate the root ball of the plant that is about to be planted.

Holding the plant by its root ball, place it through the plastic into the hole. Using the trowel (or your hands if you prefer), pull the soil back into the hole around the plant, and firm gently into place.

Fold the plastic flaps back into position around the base of the plant. Then tip piles of inorganic material – slate chips or gravel – onto the plastic around the base of the plants and spread them evenly. Ensure any remaining areas of plastic are completely covered with the stones.

Scented seat

Almost everyone enjoys sitting out in the garden or lying on a lawn sunbathing. If you have a sloping garden, you can sit on a bank, but on a level site, it is possible to create a turf seat in the garden. By growing scented plants in parts of the seat, you can enjoy the feeling of grass beneath you as well as the aroma of your favourite fragrant plants.

WHAT YOU NEED

Tools: Garden canes; string; rake; press board; large knife
Materials: Cardboard template (available from some garden centres or by mail order/internet from some garden supply companies); bricks or rubble; good-quality soil; turf or grass seed; plants such as *Tanacetum vulgare*, *Tanacetum parthenium*, *Chamaemelum nobile* and *Mentha* x *piperita citrata*

Herbs or low-growing plants could be used as an alternative to grass, but these plants tend not to be as hard-wearing and contain more sap than grass does, which means that light crushing as you sit can result in green stains on clothing. In order to blend fragrance with practicality, the bulk of the seat should be covered in grass to bind the structure together, with pockets of herbs planted at various places in the seat. The herbs will release aroma when brushed against while the seat is in use, but pose no danger to clothing. Select plants that are able to tolerate clipping at roughly the same rate as the grass that covers the seat.

Herbs such as chamomile (*Chamaemelum nobile*), eau-de-Cologne mint (*Mentha* x *piperita citrata*) and thyme (*Thymus vulgaris*) release aromatic oils that can have a very relaxing effect when drifting in the air close by. Other herbs, such as feverfew (*Tanacetum parthenium*), pennyroyal (*Mentha pulegium*) and tansy (*Tanacetum vulgare*), are natural insect repellents and the aromas they release will help to ward off the biting and stinging insects that can be such persistent pests on a warm summer evening.

Tip: It is important to remember that this type of seat will gradually settle as it becomes established. Allow for this settlement by constructing the seat slightly higher than you actually require it to be.

Mark a 1.5m (5ft) diameter circle using canes and a length of string. This circle will form the base of the seat. Rake the area level and walk over it several times to compact the soil.

Assemble the cardboard template according to the manufacturer's instructions. Make sure that each section is firmly fixed to its adjoining sections so that the structure is stable.

Fill each of the pockets in the template with bricks or rubble until the pockets are about two-thirds full. This packing material gives the seat structural strength when the cardboard decays and helps to improve drainage.

Fill the remaining portion of the pockets with good-quality soil and pat it down with a press board to firm it into place. If the soil is slightly moist, it will bond together more easily.

Lay sections of turf over the surface area of the seat and cut away any surplus turf so that a close fit can be achieved. Alternatively, sow grass seed over the surface of the soil and allow it to germinate and grow.

Plant scented plants into the arms of the chair. Select plants that are able to tolerate clipping at roughly the same rate as the grass that covers the seat.

Harvesting & drying flowers

Although plants are grown primarily to decorate the garden, the life of many flowers can be prolonged by storing them for use in dry displays to brighten up the house during winter. It is possible to preserve certain flowers so that they retain their natural fragrance as well as their form and colour. The flower heads of lavender (*Lavandula*), which is used in this project, can retain their scent long after flowering has finished.

WHAT YOU NEED
Tools: Secateurs; elastic bands; nails or hooks
Materials: Plants such as *Lavandula angustifolia*

Although the flower heads of some plants, such as *Allium*, will dry naturally if they are left on the plant, it can be an unsatisfactory process if they are battered by the weather. Much better results can be obtained if the heads are cut and preserved while they are in peak condition. Ideally, flowers should be cut on a fine, dry day just before they become fully open. Do not collect them when the air is damp or they are still covered with morning dew because they will become mouldy and discoloured rather than dry properly.

Almost any flower can be air-dried but some are more difficult than others. It is also a slow process, often taking several weeks. The best method involves hanging the flowers upside down in small, loose bunches (tied tightly at the base) in a dry, well-ventilated place. They should be kept out of direct sunlight because the sun would cause the flowers to fade. After drying, the bunches can then be removed from the drying area, sorted and rebunched, and stored until needed by hanging them in a cool, dry place such as a garage or shed.

> **Tip:** Some species of lavender may shed their flowers as they dry. To avoid losing the flowers, place a paper bag over them while they are drying.

The lavender is ready to be cut when the flowers are half to three-quarters open. They will continue to open while they are drying.

Choose a warm, sunny day when the surface of the whole plant, particularly the flowers, is dry. This will prevent mould from developing. Cut the stems with sharp secateurs to avoid bruising the stem or flower stalk.

Working on a clean, flat surface, sort through the flower stalks, stripping off the leaves and discarding any bruised or broken stems.

Grade and sort the stems for size and length, gathering 15–20 stems together. Tie them firmly with an elastic band. Do not use string because it would work loose as the stems dry and shrink.

Hang the complete bunches from nails or hooks in a dry, cool, dark place with good ventilation. Leave them for 2–4 weeks, depending on the plants being dried and how dry the atmosphere is.

When the stems are completely dry, sort through the bunches again and remove any withered flowers and stems before bunching the lavender into bouquets of about 80–100 stems.

Naturalising bulbs

Bulbs seldom grow individually in the wild but instead are found as clumps or carpets. There is no reason why we cannot imitate this in the garden, rather than planting them in regimented rows. Clumps of bulbs in a border or under a tree will create a natural effect as well as attract the eye. The fragrance will also be much stronger where flowers are massed together. The clump will need to be divided eventually, because as the bulbs reproduce and spread, they will begin to restrict one other. This can be done by lifting the entire clump after flowering as the foliage dies down and replanting it as several smaller clumps.

Bulb carpets

Carpets of bulbs can be planted wherever space allows. They look particularly good beneath deciduous trees, where they can flower while the tree is bare. This gives them the light levels they need to bloom, but they can lie dormant while the tree is in leaf and the light levels are low.

Aim to match the bulb to the situation to gain the best effect, using large flowers such as daffodils (*Narcissus*) where there is plenty of room – large flowers would be in scale in a large area but they would dominate a small garden. Conversely, small flowers like *Crocus* are difficult to see in a large area but would be perfectly in scale with a small lawn.

Naturalising in grass

If you decide to plant the bulbs to come up through grass, try to match the bulb to the conditions. Tiny bulbs will not have the ability to push their way through very coarse turf with thickly matted roots and, in this instance, a large variety would stand more chance of survival. Smaller bulbs are better suited to a fine grass mixture, which will have a less dense root system.

Naturalising in borders

Bulbs can be planted in borders to give a splash of colour and fragrance whenever their surroundings need a boost. Spring bulbs, like *Narcissus*, will flower while deciduous shrubs are still leafless and before herbaceous perennials have begun the new season's growth. Summer bulbs, such as *Allium*, will complement surrounding flowers, adding an element of height to low planting. Autumn-flowering bulbs, including *Cyclamen hederifolium*, *Colchicum* and *Crocus tommasinianus*, lie dormant through the hot, dry months of summer, when the neighbouring plants cast shade, and flower as the leaves fall and allow more light in.

Feeding

Remove the flowers as soon as they die (to stop seed from setting) and begin to feed the bulbs with 30g per square metre (1oz per square yard) of sulphate of potassium. This will help replenish the

This onion-scented Allium cristophii *seed head is growing among a patch of fennel (*Foeniculum vulgare*), which has an aniseed fragrance.*

Narcissus *look delightful when naturalised in their surroundings and their fragrance will have a stronger impact if they are planted* en masse.

food the bulb used in order to produce the flower. The leaves and remaining flower stem will continue to feed the bulb until the foliage dies down. Feeding before the flower fades makes the stem weak and floppy, ruining the flower.

Aftercare

It is important for the health of the bulbs that they are allowed to die down naturally after flowering, which takes six to eight weeks. This replenishes the food reserve within the bulb, ready to produce flowers for the following year. If this is not allowed to happen, the flowers will be of poorer quality or may not be present at all.

If you have planted bulbs in an area of turf, the grass among the leaves cannot be cut until the leaves have turned brown (bear this in mind when choosing where to plant your bulbs because this may not be acceptable on a particularly fine lawn area). Once they have turned brown, the leaves can be removed by hand or mown off with the rest of the grass.

Planting bulbs

Plant fragrant spring-flowering bulbs in mid- to late autumn. The planting and aftercare of bulbs is relatively straightforward but, contrary to popular belief, there is more to growing them than simply digging a hole in the soil and dropping a bulb into it. Attention to detail when planting is important and can mean the difference between success and failure.

WHAT YOU NEED
Tools: Bulb planting tool
Materials: Bulbs

The bulbs found in most gardens have been propagated in the same country or region as the garden. Some, however, may have originated from as far afield as South Africa, South America, the Mediterranean or the Middle East, and this will have an effect on the conditions the bulbs require in order to flourish. Start by selecting the right plant for your particular situation. Most bulbs prefer a sunny position but a few, such as bluebells (*Hyacinthoides non-scripta*) and snowdrops (*Galanthus*), prefer the dappled shade provided by trees. Many bulbs are ideal for planting under deciduous trees because they are dormant when the trees are in full leaf, and flower when the trees are dormant and the light levels are better. Most soil types are suitable for the majority of bulbs, but try to ensure that the soil is not waterlogged during the winter or the bulb may rot.

Planting depth is particularly important because inconsistent planting will lead to uneven flowering, which can spoil the effect of mass groupings of bulbs. Depending on the bulbs being planted, the depth can vary from as shallow as 1cm (½in) to as deep as 25cm (10in). It is preferable to use some form of tool for making the planting hole, but because of the wide variation in planting depth, no single tool is ideal for all bulbs.

Tip: Bulbs that are naturalised in the lawn should be left for at least six weeks after flowering before you cut down the foliage. In the meantime, you will have to mow around them. To simplify this task, group the bulbs together so that there are fewer areas to mow around.

Scatter a handful of bulbs over the desired area. This will help you achieve a random, natural look that is particularly suitable for a group of bulbs growing in grass. Plant the bulbs where they land.

Push the bulb planting tool into the ground with a twisting motion (this is much easier than trying to force the planter into the ground vertically). Still twisting, pull the planter out of the ground, removing a core of soil with it.

You can use a hand bulb planter (as pictured in step 2) or, for harder ground, an upright spade-type bulb planter will make the work much easier.

Place the bulb into the hole in an upright position, but do not press it down too firmly or, as the roots develop, they will push against the soil and force the bulb out of the ground.

Break up most of the core of the soil plug you removed in the bulb planting tool. Place the soil back in the hole around the bulb until it is level with the top of the bulb.

Place the remainder of the soil plug on top of the hole and press it gently into the ground using your gardening shoe or boot.

Fragrant hedges

Hedges can be used in a variety of ways around the garden to fulfil different functions, including marking boundaries, dividing the garden into sections, providing screens for increased privacy and acting as a windbreak. If you are using container-grown plants such as lavender (*Lavandula*), the best times to plant are autumn and spring. In autumn, the soil is still warm enough for the plant to make some root growth before it stops growing for the winter. In spring, the soil will be warming up again and the plant will soon begin to send out new roots. Bare-root plants, such as privet (*Ligustrum*), can be bought in bundles from late autumn until early spring and can be planted as soon as the weather allows.

Boundary demarcation

Hedges can be used to form a living barrier around the perimeter of your property. This may be preferable to having a solid boundary such as a wall or fence. Much will depend on your particular property and whether there are any restrictions on what can and cannot be built (check with your local authority). A hedge can be used in conjunction with a solid structure if, for instance, the wall is not as high as you would like.

Screening

If all or part of your garden is overlooked, a hedge may be the answer to gaining some privacy without building a solid barrier. A short, aromatic hedge around the sitting or dining area may be sufficient to create a feeling of privacy. You can also use hedging to hide parts of the garden that are less attractive, such as the area where you keep the dustbins or compost heap.

Wind protection

If your garden is subject to strong winds, your plants will not thrive. Even light winds can cause scorching and distorted or damaged growth. To appreciate the fragrance of the plants you are introducing, the air should be calm as often as possible. Solid barriers, like walls, cause turbulence inside the garden because the wind is diverted over the top of the wall and then swirls down inside the garden. Hedges allow some of the wind to pass through so that the flow of air is reduced to manageable levels.

Dividing into sections

Low or medium hedges can be used to mark out different areas within the garden, edge paths and guide people as they walk around. They can even be utilised to separate the garden into different sections, or 'rooms', if the garden is large enough.

Growth habit

When you are planning the hedge, you need to decide whether it is to be formal or informal, in keeping with the rest of the design. This will have an influence over which plants you can use in a particular situation because the growth habit will dictate how it will respond to pruning. Box (*Buxus sempervirens*) has a dense, twiggy habit and can be clipped into formal geometric shapes, whereas lavender (*Lavandula*) does not respond well to excessive pruning and is better suited to informal hedging.

This clever design intersperses shaped hedging with areas of fragrant planting, creating both visual and aromatic interest.

*Lavender (*Lavandula*) has a bushy habit that makes it ideal for growing as a fragrant hedge in an informal-style garden.*

Pruning

If the hedge is being grown for its aromatic leaves, you can prune it regularly to reduce its size and maintain the shape of the hedge without affecting the production of fragrance. If the plants have been selected for their flowers, however, the timing of the pruning is much more critical so that you do not remove the buds or flowers before their best display. A plant such as *Chaenomeles* flowers in early spring and produces fragrant fruits in autumn, so it is best pruned straight after flowering to allow it the full year to make more flowering growth. You will be sacrificing some fruits but, over time, regular pruning will result in a bushy, dense plant that will fruit heavily.

Planting a fragrant hedge

Hedges serve all sorts of purposes within the garden – they make excellent screens and barriers, and they provide a habitat for birds and other wildlife and a natural backdrop for other plants in the garden. A number of coniferous plants with aromatic foliage are ideal for hedging and will provide fragrance when the weather is warm and particularly when the hedge is being trimmed.

WHAT YOU NEED
Tools: Garden line; measuring rod; spade; wheelbarrow
Materials: Conifer plants; organic mulch

Coniferous evergreen plants are excellent for providing year-round shelter (particularly where walls and fences are not practical) as well as fragrance when planted as hedging. Some, like *Thuja plicata* 'Zebrina', have a sweet resinous aroma and the advantage of attractive green- and gold-variegated foliage; others, such as *Thuja occidentalis*, produce a resinous, pineapple scent.

The best time for planting depends on the plants being used. Deciduous plants are cheaper bought 'bare-root' in bundles for planting between late autumn and early spring, while broad-leaved evergreens and conifers are usually available as 'container-grown' plants that can be planted in early autumn or late spring.

Remember that a hedge is a long-term planting and the soil should be well-prepared beforehand. The plants will need trimming regularly for the first few years to encourage the growth to become thick and bushy at the base.

Tip: To get the best effect from a fragrant hedge, grow it in a formal design, keeping it quite closely clipped to the desired height and outline. The hedging plants should be trimmed at least once a year, more often (two or three times a year) with some of the more vigorous plants.

Start by marking out the course of the hedge with a garden line. To get accurate spacings between the plants, make a measuring rod with the plant spacings marked on it from a section of wooden batten.

Using a spade, dig out the hole for the first plant, and place the soil in a wheelbarrow (this soil can be taken to the end of the hedge line and used to fill the final planting hole).

Remove the plant from its container and position it in the planting hole, making sure the root ball of the plant is at the correct height.

Dig out the hole for the second plant, and put the soil from this second hole around the roots of the plant in the first planting hole.

Adjust the level of the plant's roots (if necessary) and firm the soil in the planting hole with the heel of a boot or shoe. Repeat steps 3, 4 and 5 until the hedge is completed.

Finally, remove the garden line and cover the soil with a layer of well-rotted organic mulch to suppress weeds and retain moisture.

TREES

KEY INFORMATION

H: The average height the plant can reach

S: The average spread the plant can achieve

Sun/partial shade/shade: The position the plant prefers

Well-drained/moderate/moist: How much water the plant needs

Acid/alkaline/neutral/any: The plant's preferred soil type

Z1 to Z10: The minimum winter temperature (zone) the plant can withstand

Zone 1: below –46°C (below –50°F)
Zone 2: –46 to –40°C (–50 to –40°F)
Zone 3: –40 to –34°C (–40 to –30°F)
Zone 4: –34 to –29°C (–30 to –20°F)
Zone 5: –29 to –23°C (–20 to –10°F)
Zone 6: –23 to –18°C (–10 to 0°F)
Zone 7: –18 to –12°C (0 to 10°F)
Zone 8: –12 to –7°C (10 to 20°F)
Zone 9: –7 to –1°C (20 to 30°F)
Zone 10: –1 to 4°C (30 to 40°F)

Arbutus unedo
H 8m (26ft) S 8m (26ft)
Sun
Moderate
Acid/neutral Z7

This attractive, slow-growing, broad-leaved evergreen forms an open, spreading, sometimes shrubby tree. It has deep brown bark that peels off to reveal the new green bark beneath. The white urn-shaped flowers are honey-scented and produced in large hanging trusses on the tips of the branches in autumn. These are followed by orange-red fruits that take a year to ripen. There is also a form with dark pink flowers, *A. u. rubra*. Propagate by taking semi-ripe cuttings in late summer and placing them in a cold frame to root over winter.

Magnolia grandiflora
H 10m (32ft) S 5m (16ft)
Sun
Moderate
Acid/neutral Z6

This small tree is one of the best magnolias. The glossy evergreen leaves are up to 20cm (8in) long and have an orange-brown, felt-like covering on the undersides. From mid-summer until mid-autumn, large, bowl-shaped, creamy yellow flowers up to 25cm (10in) across and with between 9 and 12 petals are borne on the tips of shoots. The cultivar *M. g.* 'Exmouth' has richly fragrant flowers. Prune only to maintain the health and shape of the plant. Propagate by taking semi-ripe cuttings in summer or by layering shoots in autumn and severing them from the parent plant one or two years later.

Parrotia persica
H 8m (26ft) S 10m (32ft)
Sun/partial shade
Well-drained
Acid Z5

This small deciduous tree is closely
related to *Hamamelis*. It has a
wide- spreading habit and is grown
mainly for its attractive autumn
leaf colour. The leaves are roughly
oval in shape with a rounded base
and are mid-green in spring and
summer, turning crimson and
gold in autumn. Small, crimson,
delicately scented flowers appear in
late winter to early spring before the
leaves emerge. The bark of mature
plants flakes off in patches to reveal
interesting patterns in winter. There
is also a weeping form of this tree,
P. p. 'Pendula'. Propagate by taking
softwood cuttings in summer or
sowing seed in autumn.

Plumeria rubra
H 7m (20ft) S 5m (15ft)
Sun
Moderate
Any Z10

The common frangipani is a
small deciduous tree with an
upright habit, consisting of a few
sparse but thick branches. It is ideal
for the conservatory, where its size
can be controlled by growing it in
a container. The mid-green leaves
are broadly lance-shaped and
arranged alternately along the
stems. In summer and autumn,
clusters of strongly jasmine-scented,
yellow-eyed flowers are produced.
The flowers, which are up to 10cm
(4in) across with rounded yellow,
red or bronze petals, adopt a flat,
open shape as they develop. This
plant can be grown in a container
and moved indoors for winter
protection. Propagate by sowing
seed at a temperature of 18°C
(64°F) in the spring.

***Prunus subhirtella* 'Autumnalis Rosea'**
H 8m (26ft) S 8m (26ft)
Sun
Moderate
Any Z6

This deciduous tree has an open,
spreading habit and broadly oval-
shaped, dark green leaves with
sharply toothed margins, tinted
purple when they emerge in spring
and turning a dull golden yellow
in autumn before they fall. This
remarkable tree hardly stops
flowering between autumn and
spring. The flowers fade and open in
steady succession and there is rarely
a time when the tree does not have
some semi-double rose-pink flowers
that carry a sweet almond scent,
although it is rarely totally covered.
Propagate by budding in summer
or grafting in winter.

SHRUBS

Abelia x _grandiflora_
H 3m (10ft) S 4m (13ft)
Sun
Moderate
Any Z5

This hybrid shrub of garden origin has glossy, oval-shaped, semi-evergreen leaves carried on thin, twiggy branches, giving the plant a loose, spreading appearance. In late summer and throughout autumn, attractive tubular flowers are borne in open clusters on the shoot tips. They are lightly fragrant and coloured soft pink fading to white with age. A less vigorous form, _A._ x _grandiflora_ 'Francis Mason', is a better choice for smaller gardens. Some protection may be necessary in severe winters. Propagate by taking 10cm- (4in)-long tip cuttings in summer and placing them in a cold frame.

Buddleja davidii
H 3m (10ft) S 5m (16ft)
Sun
Moderate
Any Z5

This vigorous shrub has an open, spreading habit, producing long, arching stems, and is commonly known as the butterfly bush because of the insects it attracts. The lance-shaped, grey-green leaves are up to 25cm (10in) long, with a light felt-like covering when young. In late summer through until late autumn, 30cm (12in) long spikes of lilac to purple or purple-red fragrant flowers are produced on the tips of the branches, followed by later, smaller flowers from the lateral shoots. There are a number of excellent named cultivars, including 'Black Knight' and 'Peace'. Propagate by taking hardwood cuttings from leafless stems in winter.

Buddleja x _weyeriana_ 'Sungold'
H 4m (12ft) S 3m (10ft)
Sun
Moderate
Any Z6

A hybrid between _B. davidii_ and _B. globosa_, this deciduous shrub has an open spreading habit. Its arching brownish green stems carry opposite pairs of lance-shaped silvery green leaves, which are covered in a dense greyish felt when young. The tips of the stems bear 30cm (12in) long flower spikes with large numbers of tiny fragrant flowers, each with an orange centre, which open golden yellow and fade to yellowish pink. Propagation is by semi-ripe cuttings taken from side shoots in the summer.

Choisya ternata
H 1.5m (5ft) S 1.5m (5ft)
Sun
Moderate
Any Z7

The Mexican orange blossom is a
compact, evergreen shrub with
glossy, aromatic, palmate leaves
produced in whorls on green,
woody stems. Dense clusters of
small, white, musk-scented, star-
shaped flowers appear in late spring
and again in late summer and
autumn. C. t. 'Sundance' rarely
flowers but has bright yellow foliage
(although this may scorch in intense
sunlight and turns lime-green in
partial shade). C. 'Aztec Pearl' is
compact, with long, thin, dark green
leaflets and pink-tinted white
flowers. Grow in any well-drained
soil or a container and prune only
to remove any damaged shoots.
Propagate by taking semi-ripe
cuttings in late summer.

Elaeagnus x ebbingei
H 3m (10ft) S 3m (10ft)
Sun
Well-drained/moderate
Any Z6

This is an attractive, hardy and
reliable evergreen shrub, tolerant of
coastal exposure, with a spreading
habit and scaly, golden bronze
shoots. The leathery, broadly lance-
shaped leaves are metallic green
above and silvery green beneath.
In autumn and winter, small, highly
fragrant, bell-like white flowers are
produced beneath the leaves. The
fragrance is often noticed before
the flowers are seen. Variegated
cultivars include 'Gilt Edge'
(yellow-edged leaves) and
'Limelight' (silvery new shoots and
lime-green to yellow leaf markings).
Remove any shoots that revert to
green on a variegated plant or they
will take over. Propagate by taking
semi-ripe cuttings in summer.

Myrtus communis
H 3m (10ft) S 3m (10ft)
Sun
Well-drained/moderate
Any Z8

The myrtle is a bushy shrub with
dense foliage and an upright habit,
with the branches arching as the
plant ages. The oval, aromatic
leaves are glossy dark green and
about 5cm (2in) long, arranged in
opposite pairs along orange-brown
stems. From late summer into
autumn, the five-petalled white
flowers have a pronounced central
tuft of stamens and are sweetly
scented. They are borne singly on
the branches and are often followed
by strongly aromatic, purple-black
fruits in late autumn. There are a
number of variegated forms,
including M. c. 'Variegata'.
Propagate by taking semi-ripe
cuttings in late summer or sowing
seed in a cold frame in autumn.

SHRUBS

Osmanthus armatus
H 5m (16ft) S 4m (13ft)
Sun/partial shade
Well-drained
Any Z7

This is a rounded shrub with a
dense habit, often spreading with
age. It has large, lance-shaped
evergreen leaves with a sharp,
spiny-toothed margin. The leaves
are a shiny dark green with a tough,
leathery texture, measuring up to
15cm (6in) in length. The creamy
white, broadly tubular flowers are
very sweetly scented and carried
in clusters at the base of each leaf
joint on young branching stems
in autumn. The flowers are often
followed by 2–3cm (1in) long
oval-shaped berries that are dark
violet in colour. Propagate by
sowing seed in a cold frame as
soon as it is ripe or by taking
semi-ripe cuttings in summer.

Osmanthus heterophyllus
H 5m (16ft) S 5m (16ft)
Sun/partial shade
Moderate
Any Z6

Originating from Japan, this slow-
growing shrub with a rounded,
spreading habit is often mistaken
for holly. The mid-green leaves have
a leathery texture and are broadly
elliptical in shape, about 6cm (2½in)
long, with a row of spines along the
margin. The leaves are often absent
on the new stems of mature plants.
In early autumn, small fragrant
tubular flowers are produced in
small clusters in the axils of the
leaves and stem, followed by oval,
bluish-black fruits. Propagate by
sowing seed in a cold frame as soon
as it is ripe or by taking semi-ripe
cuttings in summer.

Yucca gloriosa
H 2.5m (8ft) S 2m (7ft)
Sun
Well-drained/moderate
Neutral Z7

A native of the south-eastern United
States, this striking hardy evergreen
shrub thrives in poor sandy
conditions. The long strap-like
leaves are a bluish-green in colour,
maturing to dark green. They are
usually dried and brown at the tip
to form a sharp, spine-like point. In
late summer and into autumn, the
spectacular flower spikes are often
2.5m (8ft) high and covered with
white, drooping, bell-shaped, lily-
like blooms, each up to 5cm (2in)
long. The cultivar Y. g. 'Nobilis'
often has red markings on the
petals. Propagate by removing and
planting rooted suckers in spring.

CLIMBERS & WALL SHRUBS

Lonicera japonica
H 10m (32ft) S 10m (32ft)
Sun/partial shade
Well-drained/moderate
Any Z4

This attractive honeysuckle has
twining stems with evergreen to
semi-evergreen leaves that are
broadly oval in shape, glossy green
in colour and carried in pairs on
thin, twiggy stems. The fragrant
flowers are tubular, opening out
to a broad mouth, and are carried
individually or in small clusters.
They are a purple-tinged white
when they first appear and age to a
deep yellow. By late autumn as the
flowers fade, small blue to black
fruits are produced. Prune by cutting
back lateral shoots in spring and
remove some of the older wood to
allow room for younger shoots to
develop. Propagate by taking
hardwood cuttings in winter.

Passiflora caerulea
H 6.5m (22ft) S 5m (16ft)
Sun
Well-drained/moderate
Any Z7

The passion flower is a climbing
perennial that will die down for the
winter in all but the mildest areas
and emerge as vigorous as ever the
following spring. From late summer
into autumn, the beautiful, large,
fragrant flowers are borne singly on
short green stalks. They have large
pink-white sepals and petals, with
spiky blue filaments tinged white
and purple in the centre of the
bloom. The palm-shaped leaves
have 5–7 fingers, are mid-green in
colour and are carried on square,
green stems. The plant supports itself
by using thin green tendrils and can
grow up to 6.5m (22ft) in length
within a season. Propagate by taking
heel cuttings in mid- to late summer.

Rosa 'Mermaid'
H 7m (23ft) S 7m (23ft)
Sun
Moderate
Any Z5

One of the most useful and
beautiful climbing roses, this
vigorous plant has long, arching
stems. The large, glossy green
leaves are practically evergreen,
carried on brownish-maroon wood
and well armed with large, curved
thorns, red when young and turning
brown with age. The large, single,
primrose-yellow flowers are often
10cm (4in) across when fully open,
revealing a huge cluster of golden-
brown stamens in the centre of each
bloom. These fragrant flowers are
produced from mid-summer until
well into autumn, stopping only
when the first frosts arrive.
Propagate by budding in summer
or grafting in winter.

PERENNIALS, ANNUALS & BIENNIALS

Achillea filipendulina
H 1.2m (4ft) S 45cm (18in)
Sun
Moderate
Any Z3

Commonly known as yarrow,
this herbaceous perennial has a
compact, upright habit, with broad,
finely divided, slightly hairy leaves
that are a dull green in colour.
The lemon-yellow flowers are held
erect above the foliage in bold flat
clusters 13–15cm (5–6in) across
from late summer until early
autumn. One very popular form is
A. f. 'Gold Plate', which has deep
golden yellow flowers. The finely
cut foliage has a pungent aroma
(feverfew) and is excellent for use
in potpourri. These plants are also
popular with flower arrangers.
Propagate by lifting the clumps in
spring, dividing them into smaller
portions of 4–5 shoots and
replanting them.

Coriandrum sativum
H 60cm (2ft) S 30cm (12in)
Sun/partial shade
Well-drained
Any Z7

Coriander is a hardy annual
originating from the Mediterranean
with long-stalked, fern-like, glossy
dark green foliage that produces
a strong citrus aroma. From mid-
summer until late autumn, broad
flat clusters of small cup-shaped
white or pale purple flowers about
5cm (2in) across are produced on
the tips of shoots. The flowers are
followed by pale golden brown
fruits that emit an orange-like scent
when dried. Propagate by sowing
seed directly into the soil outdoors
in late spring.

Lilium speciosum
H 1–1.5m (3–5ft) S 30cm (12in)
Partial shade
Moist
Acid Z5

This well-known species produces
flowers that are so fragrant they
are often sold as cut flowers. The
rounded bulbs are yellowish to
purple-brown in colour and produce
erect green stems, often with purple
markings along their length, and
carry evenly scattered, broadly
lance-shaped, mid-green leaves.
From mid-summer through autumn,
the large flowers protrude
horizontally from the main stem,
with the individual blooms having
strongly reflexed, wavy-margined
petals that are basically white with
deeper pink centres. There are some
colour variants, such as L. s. var.
album, with pure white flowers,
and L. s. var. rubrum, with deep
carmine-red flowers. Propagate by
lily scaling or dividing in autumn.

PERENNIALS, ANNUALS & BIENNIALS

Nerine bowdenii
H 75cm (30in) S 8cm (3in)
Sun
Well-drained
Any Z8

Originating from South Africa, this sturdy, bulbous, hardy herbaceous perennial produces clusters of broad, semi-erect, strap-shaped mid-green leaves that often appear as the flowers open. In autumn, open clusters of funnel-shaped, lily-like, scented pink flowers with a frilled edge to the petals are produced above the leaves on slender green stalks. There is also a very attractive white-flowered form of this plant, *Nerine bowdenii* f. *alba*. Propagate by sowing seed as soon as it is ripe or dividing established clumps after they have finished flowering.

Romneya coulteri
H 1.2m (4ft) S 2m (7ft)
Sun
Well-drained
Alkaline/neutral Z7

This shrubby herbaceous perennial, originates from California and is commonly named the Californian poppy. It has blue-green, broad oval leaves that are deeply lobed, looking almost like large fern leaves, and carried on thick blue-green stems. It is grown for its huge white poppy flowers, 10–13cm (4–5in) across, with a large cluster of golden stamens and a sweet, exotic perfume. The flowers appear from late summer well into autumn. Another species, *R. trichocalyx*, is slightly smaller and less vigorous than *R. coulteri* but produces flowers that are much more fragrant during the summer months. Propagate by taking root cuttings in late winter or early spring.

Scabiosa atropurpurea
H 1m (3ft) S 25cm (10in)
Sun
Moderate
Alkaline/neutral Z9

Commonly known as the pincushion flower or sweet scabious, this is a hardy biennial with large, solitary, chrysanthemum-like flowers ranging from purple to lilac in colour and with a honey scent. They are borne on long, slender, pale green leafless stems from mid-summer into autumn. The leaves are strap-like, with the upper part divided into narrow segments, and form a low matted cluster reaching no more than 20–30cm (8–12in) high. The flowers grow above the foliage and are excellent as cut flowers. Propagate by sowing seed indoors in early spring or outdoors in late spring.

chapter six

6

Plants for winter

Some of the most fragrant plants flower through the winter months, producing blooms of outstanding scent and beauty. Some of these flowers are delicate in appearance but are capable of withstanding all but the most bitter winter weather conditions. By selecting a range of plants, you can achieve a continuous array of fragrances throughout winter, but take care not to overdo it. Too many scented plants positioned close together and flowering at the same time will spoil the effect because the fragrances will overlap one another. Although the beauty of the flowers can be appreciated, each individual fragrance will be lost in a cloud of pleasant but indistinguishable scents.

Winter scent

Each species has its own way of attracting pollinators at this time of year, when the insect population is low. Plants competing for the same pollinators will use different fragrances as attractants. Winter-flowering jasmine (*Jasminum nudiflorum*) has honey-scented flowers, *Mahonia japonica* has a lily-of-the-valley type of fragrance and *Daphne odora* has a spicy scent. A wider range of fragrances can be found among *Viburnum*, with different species having the scent of cloves, jonquil, heliotrope or a sweet scent. However, to give the impression that all winter-flowering plants are heavily and pleasantly scented would be wrong. Some have no scent while others have a pronounced unpleasant smell. For example, the winter-flowering *Helleborus foetidus* is commonly called the stinking hellebore because of its strong aroma, and *Daphne laureola* produces an unpleasant odour.

Tall plants

It is important to strike a balance when positioning winter plants, so that you can smell the flowers when they are in bloom but you do not have to go to great lengths disguising the spaces they leave when they die back during the summer. Some of the taller growing plants that have a strong perfume can be a good solution to this problem. Plants such as wintersweet (*Chimonanthus praecox*), witch hazel (*Hamamelis*) and *Mahonia* need to be grown farther back in a border because of their size. If they can be grown behind lower-growing deciduous plants, so that they are seen in all of their glory through the winter months but are partially obscured during the summer months, then so much the better. However, do take all qualities into consideration; *Hamamelis* species also tend to have glorious autumn colours that you will want in full view.

Wall plants

Growing plants close to buildings can be a useful method of gaining the maximum effect from any perfume given off by their flowers, especially when they are positioned close to a window or door that is regularly opened during the flowering period so that even a small amount of the scent can be fully appreciated indoors. Plants grown close to buildings often flower slightly earlier (and for longer) than their counterparts standing farther away in the garden, because they benefit from the protection of the walls and their residual heat. Winter-flowering wall plants

Choose your winter plants with care. This Helleborus orientalis *has a mild but attractive scent – unlike the stinking* Helleborus foetidus.

include the yellow-flowered *Jasminum nudiflorum* and the ever-green climber *Clematis cirrhosa* var. *balearica*. Unfortunately, the disadvantage to this growth being slightly ahead of the season is that, if a period of cold sets in, these plants are usually casualties and a whole season's flowers and fragrance can be lost overnight.

Bulbs

Bulbs with fragrant flowers look best when planted outdoors in large drifts or groups. This allows the fragrance to make a real impact and is particularly important with small, low-growing bulbs such as *Crocus* and hardy *Cyclamen*. It is easier to let the fragrance rise up to meet you from a large group of flowers than have to stoop to catch the scent of a few blooms.

Hyacinthus and *Narcissus* bulbs and *Crocus* corms can be 'forced' in bowls to bring them into flower indoors earlier than they would outside (see pages 64–65). These attractive blooms, particularly *Hyacinthus* and some of the *Narcissus*, are valued as much for their heavy perfume as their colour. Forcing these plants to flower ahead of their natural season not only provides interest over the quieter winter period but, with successional plantings, can provide colour and fragrance well into the spring.

Indoor fragrance

Fragrance does not have to be confined to the garden, and many scented winter-flowering shrubs can be used as cut flowers, with stems of partly opened flowers brought indoors and placed in water. In the warmth of a room, these flowers will open and gradually envelop the room with a cloud of fragrance, often for a week or more before they need to be replaced.

Winter weather and its effects

The weather is more unreliable in winter than at any other time and can range from heavy, lying snow that smothers the plants, to prolonged rainfall, bitingly cold winds and frost, depending upon where you live. In coastal areas, the conditions will be made less extreme by the influence of the sea and you will rarely get frost, but fog will make the air moist and the winds will be salt-laden. Although deciduous trees and shrubs look dead when they lose their leaves in the winter, the plants have simply withdrawn nutrients back into themselves for protection from the cold weather. They do in fact continue to grow very slowly. Their roots are active throughout (except for a very short period in the middle of winter) and changes take place in the shoots so that, as soon as the weather warms up, the buds will be ready to burst open and the new leaves unfurl or the flowers open.

Jobs for winter

There is no point gardening in winter, is there? Isn't everything dead? It is a season of frosts and cold that is hardly likely to promote outdoor activity. However, this is a misconception because winter is no different from any other season. It is just that the weather is colder and the growth rate of most plants slows down. Although many of the fragrant plants grown in the garden are resting through the winter months, the gardener is far from inactive and, in many respects, winter in the garden can be as busy as any other season of the year.

Plant care

Check the greenhouse or cold frame constantly for signs of pests or diseases, which take advantage of the protection. Pay attention to hygiene and remove plant debris to cut the risk of infection, particularly if you are reluctant to use chemical controls. Plants that are actively growing in a greenhouse, house or conservatory need dead flower heads removing, along with any yellowing leaves, before mould starts to grow. Careful water management will ensure that flowering and growth is not impaired by over- or under-watering. Woody indoor plants, such as *Citrus*, tend to produce soft, sappy growth if they are growing in a warm environment with poor winter light levels, and some pruning may be required to keep the growth balanced.

Heavy snowfalls can settle on plants, particularly conifers and evergreens with a larger surface area, and the weight can cause branches to bend or break. Knock the snow off these to help reduce damage, because a torn branch leaves an open wound for infections to enter in spring.

Protection

Save energy by insulating greenhouses and cold frames with bubble plastic or similar. Reducing draughts will save on heat loss and plant casualties. Outdoors, new plants introduced since the previous winter will need protection if the weather turns severe. Wind tends to be the real killer, rather than low temperatures. Evergreens, plants growing in containers and tall plants, including any over 45cm (18in) that have not been firmly anchored, are the most vulnerable. They can be severely damaged by wind-rock, which loosens the roots, and need to be re-firmed and staked or protected. If your garden is particularly windswept, you may wish to consider planting a windbreak of some sort to reduce the airflow. Creating shelter in the garden will also allow you to appreciate the fragrance of the plants more in the calmer air.

Another problem that the wind causes for these plants is the foliage drying out. Conifers and broad-leaved evergreens suffer wind-chill damage when freezing winds draw moisture from leaves faster than it can be replaced, resulting in brown, dry foliage on the windward side. When the garden soil is wet or frozen, the roots are unable to take up water to replace the moisture drawn out of the leaves by the wind. A screen of woven plastic mesh or horticultural fleece on the windward side of the plant will reduce the wind's effects and protect the leaves.

During heavy frosts, some plants may benefit from being wrapped in protective fleece, so that it absorbs at least some of the cold. Plants growing in containers need their roots protecting from the cold, either by insulating the container or temporarily moving the whole plant into a more sheltered environment.

Soil preparation

Soil improvement is a winter job because there are areas of bare soil that are only found between plantings. The heavier the soil, the more important it is to dig in early autumn, because winter frost can break down sticky clay soil better than any cultivation tool. For heavy soils, winter frost is an ally rather than an enemy, and the incorporation of compost or other organic matter will benefit both the soil structure and the plants growing in it for years to come.

Construction

Winter is a good time for dealing with construction and landscaping jobs, when sections of the garden may be bare. It is easier to see the garden layout and make changes for the coming spring. If the soil is not too wet to be structurally damaged by foot traffic and wheelbarrows, drainage systems can be installed or improved. Although summer is often regarded as the best time for installing drains in a heavy clay soil, the ground can be rock solid at that time of year, as well as occupied by plants.

Repairs and maintenance

Repairs and maintenance figure prominently during winter when the lack of vegetation is a bonus. For instance, this is an ideal time to drain and clean pools and ponds, and carry out running repairs to pond sides, walls and liners, while the plants are dormant and the fish lethargic.

The lawn will benefit from attention during late winter and early spring before new growth starts – re-levelling, changing the shape, increasing the shape and size of borders, and re-seeding areas where growth is sparse (or places where the grass has died out altogether). Remember that no work should be carried out if the grass is frozen because footprints made on frozen grass can cause it to turn brown. The reason for this is that the cells within the leaves are full of ice rather than sap in cold weather.

*Small-leaved plants, such as highly fragrant Christmas box (*Sarcococca humilis*), can cope with snowfall, but remember to shake the snow off plants with a larger surface area in case it causes them to bend and break.*

Propagation & planting

Winter can seem like a quiet time in the garden, when nothing is growing and not much is happening. However, there is still plenty of propagating and planting to do. Some seeds need to be chilled during the colder weather in order to germinate later in the year. Species of hardy plants that come true from seed can be propagated at this time, while named cultivars (which do not come true from seed) can be grown from cuttings. You may also need to transplant more established plants so that their roots can settle in during the winter, ready to grow in the coming seasons.

Growing from seed

The seeds of plants like roses (*Rosa*) need exposing to a period of cold – known as stratifying – in order to help them germinate during the following spring and summer. Sowing seed from this type of plant in late autumn allows it to be chilled to temperatures between –2 and +2°C (28 and 35°F) during the winter, causing the necessary chemical changes within the seed that will bring about germination later. Other hardy plants, such as *Hamamelis*, can also be propagated from seed at this time.

Hardwood cuttings

Winter is the ideal time to increase numbers of many of those trees and shrubs that can be propagated by hardwood cuttings. Take sections of the current season's growth and insert them into the garden soil. This method of propagation will produce new large plants within 10–12 months. If the cuttings are taken before the middle of winter, they will have started to form new roots within a month. Broad-leaved evergreen plants, like *Elaeagnus* and *Mahonia*, can be taken as cuttings and placed under protection in a cold frame to prevent them from drying out. Leave the plants in the frame for a whole year so that they have a large enough root system for transplanting.

Division

Many non-woody plants, such as herbaceous perennials, can be lifted and divided into smaller segments before being replanted. To keep these plants healthy and flowering well, this process should be repeated every 3–4 years. The most important thing is to discard any old, dead or diseased parts of the original clump. This will help to reduce pests and diseases on the older plants and stop them from being passed on to the new ones.

Transplanting

It is important to get maximum benefit from hardy winter-flowering plants because, although many are heavily scented, they may flower for a relatively short time. The period when their fragrance is at its peak is even shorter and usually falls about one-third of the way between the bud opening and the flower's death. The most obvious approach is to site the plants as close to a path or walkway as possible. Unfortunately, many of the plants that provide glorious winter colour have very little to recommend them during the rest of the year, so having them at the front of

Hardy plants such as this Hamamelis x intermedia *'Diane' can be propagated by seed during the winter months.*

During winter, take cuttings of broad-leaved evergreen plants such as this Mahonia lomariifolia *and place them in a cold frame.*

the border means having a potentially dull-looking plant in full view during other seasons. These factors must be borne in mind when making planting decisions.

Bare-root plants

The worst possible time for planting bare-root plants is when the weather is cold and windy. If the roots are subjected to drying winds for as little as 20 minutes, they will be damaged and will need to heal before the plant can start to produce new root growth and establish itself in the new position. If the soil and weather conditions are very bad, the plants can be 'heeled in' (temporarily planted in a sheltered part of the garden) and planted into their permanent site when conditions improve.

Container-grown plants

Where the garden soil is wet or heavy (clay), avoid planting container-grown plants until the soil has drained. The reason for this is that many of the loamless composts used for growing plants in containers are very absorbent and will attract water from the surrounding garden soil into the planting hole. This can lead to the plant's roots literally drowning due to lack of oxygen.

Propagating fragrant lilies

You can easily and cheaply increase the number of fragrant plants in your garden (or provide plants for friends and family) by making use of some simple propagation techniques. Lilies (*Lilium*), despite looking exotic, are in fact extremely easy to propagate. Using a simple form of leaf cutting, you can produce a large quantity of new plants and enjoy their fragrant trumpet-shaped flowers the following year.

WHAT YOU NEED

Materials: Lily bulbs; polythene bag; fine-grade sphagnum moss peat or similar compost; labels; fungicide; plant pots

A very simple form of leaf cutting is probably the easiest way to propagate lilies. Removing the outer modified leaves (scales) from the parent bulb can produce large quantities of new plants. This is a highly productive method of increasing plant numbers as it is possible to remove up to 80 per cent of the outer scales from the parent bulb, which will still grow and produce a flower the following year if it is replanted.

This method is usually practised through the autumn and into winter while the bulb is dormant, although the preparation should start earlier in the year. In late summer and early autumn (depending on the species, but definitely after flowering and as the stem begins to turn brown and dry), carefully lift the bulbs from the ground and leave them in a seed tray to dry for 2–3 days, before carefully brushing the soil from the outer scales of the bulb and removing the dead flower stem.

It is particularly important that the bulb is as clean as possible before propagation because any soil or rotting plant tissue may be a source of infection, which can rapidly spread to healthy lily scales during the warm, humid conditions while the lilies are being propagated.

Tip: Some lilies can be propagated by small, pea-sized bulblets, which form in the angle where the leaf and stem join together.

Remove the outer scales from the parent bulb by breaking them off at the point where they are attached to the basal plate of the bulb. It is important to work systematically around the bulb to avoid damaging any scales unnecessarily.

Place the scales in a polythene bag and add enough peat (or compost) so the bag contains equal amounts of peat and scales. Add the fungicide, close the bag and turn the contents over several times so that the peat, scales and fungicide are evenly mixed.

Loosely tie up the bag and label it with the plant's name and the date. Place the bag in a warm, dark place (like a clothes cupboard) for 2–3 months. Each scale should now have at least one small embryo bulb (bulblet) about 6mm (¼in) long, with white fibrous roots.

Each scale, complete with bulblets, can be potted into a small 7–8cm (3in) pot with just the tip of the old scale showing, and placed outdoors.

As the weather becomes warmer in the spring, new grass-like leaves will appear through the compost, growing from the bulblets.

In the autumn, these young bulbs can be planted in the garden soil and may flower the following year.

Taking root cuttings

Propagating plants from root cuttings can be a simple and quick way of increasing plant numbers, but it remains one of the least-known propagation techniques. It is the standard method of propagating a few plant species, mainly herbaceous perennials and alpines, but a large number of fragrant trees, shrubs and climbers can also be grown in this way.

WHAT YOU NEED
Tools: Garden fork; secateurs; sharp knife
Materials: Plants such as *Acanthus spinosus, Wisteria, Phlox, Romneya, Chaenomeles, Sassafras* and *Aesculus parviflora*; plant pots; compost; grit

The beauty of propagating plants from root cuttings is that a large number of plants can be produced from a small number of roots without disfiguring the plant, which can sometimes happen with stem cuttings. The plants that can be propagated from this type of cutting have roots containing dormant buds, which have the capacity to produce new shoots and stems. Each new plant should look identical to the parent it was taken from.

Root cuttings fall into two basic categories: cuttings from plants with thick, fleshy roots (such as *Romneya, Aesculus* and *Echinops*) that can be inserted vertically into propagating compost; and cuttings from plants with thin, wiry roots (such as *Phlox, Eryngium* – pictured here – and *Hesperis*) that are laid horizontally on top of the propagating compost. The best time to propagate plants from root cuttings is when the plant is fully dormant. This is usually in late winter and early spring. Although it is possible to take this type of cutting at other times during the plant's life cycle, the rate of success is usually much poorer.

Tip: Root cuttings can be used as a method of combating some plant pests. Some species of *Phlox*, for example, are propagated from root cuttings in an attempt to combat eelworms, which live only in the leaves and stems.

Using a garden fork, carefully dig around the roots of the plant that is to be propagated so that some roots are exposed and clearly visible.

Cut through some of the strongest and healthiest roots, using a pair of secateurs, and remove them. Replace the soil around the plant and gently firm it back into position.

Wash the roots carefully to remove as much soil as possible. This will make it easier to see where to cut, and reduces excessive wear and tear on knives and secateurs.

Using a sharp knife, cut the roots into 5cm (2in) long sections, with a flat cut (at a right angle to the root) at the top of the cutting, and a slanting cut at the bottom. This ensures that the cuttings are not inserted into the compost upside down.

If the cuttings are thick and fleshy, gently push them into a pot of compost so that the top of each cutting is level with the surface of the compost. If the cuttings are thin, lay them horizontally over the surface of the compost.

Cover the cuttings with a layer of grit. This will allow air to reach the top of the cuttings without letting them dry out. It also acts as an effective barrier against slugs.

Preparing to plant

The first step to successful planting is, of course, to select the plant carefully. Look for a well-balanced, healthy plant with evenly spaced branches and a strong structure. There should be no sign of damaged or broken branches, or any visible sign of pests and diseases. Trees and shrubs should have a wide-angled joint between the branch and stem for the main structural or framework branches. Reject any plants with excess weeds in the compost. How and when you plant will then depend on whether your fragrant plant is a container-grown, bare-root or root-balled plant.

Container-grown

Plants grown in containers can be purchased and planted at any time of year, provided the soil and weather conditions are suitable for the species. For this reason, container-grown plants are a convenient way of adding new plants to the garden. Remove the container and examine the root system of the plant, discarding any with damaged roots or excess sucker growths.

Bare-root

These are plants where all of the soil has been removed from around the roots. The roots are usually wrapped in plastic to protect them from frost or drying out. Bare-root plants are only available when the plants are dormant, ready to be planted whenever the soil and weather conditions are suitable. They tend to be cheaper than container-grown or root-balled plants.

Root-balled

Root-balled plants have soil around the roots and are tightly wrapped in burlap. They are usually available between autumn and spring and can be planted whenever conditions are suitable.

OPPOSITE *The key to successful planting is to choose plants with a well-balanced structure, such as gracefully arching* Abeliophyllum distichum.

Choose a well-balanced plant with evenly spaced branches and no damaged foliage, broken branches or stems. Remove the root wrapping and examine the root system of the plant, discarding any with rotting or damaged roots.

Staking and supporting

Newly planted trees can support themselves once the roots have anchored but will require support initially, especially in exposed positions. For bare-root trees, position the stake into the planting hole before planting. This will ensure that the tree support is firmly fixed into the soil and the roots are not damaged by knocking in the stake after planting. Even on exposed sites, the tree only needs anchoring near the base with a tie 15–20cm (6–8in) above soil level. Provided the roots are static, they can establish quickly, leaving the stem to flex in the wind and thicken naturally. Position the stake on the windward side of the tree so that it tugs at the stake rather than blowing against it, which could cause bruising or breakage. For container-grown or root-balled trees, drive the stake into the surrounding soil at an angle of about 45° to avoid damaging the plant's root system. The top of the stake should point towards the direction of the prevailing wind to ensure that the stem drives the stake farther into the ground as the wind blows it. Tie the tree to the support about 30cm (1ft) above ground level.

SELECTING YOUR FRAGRANT PLANT

TYPE OF PLANT	ADVANTAGES	DISADVANTAGES
Container-grown plants	• Available for 12 months of the year • Ideal for plants that resent root disturbance or suffer 'shock' or reduced growth after being transplanted	• More expensive, often by as much as 30–40 per cent • Often difficult to support or stake • Larger specimens can be very heavy and awkward to handle due to the volume of compost in the container
Bare-root plants	• Plants are relatively light due to lack of compost or soil around the roots • Often much easier to support or stake while planting because the roots are visible • Usually less expensive than container-grown plants	• Only available for about six months of the year (when the plant is dormant)
Root-balled plants	• Usually less expensive than container-grown plants • Better for plants such as conifers and broad-leaved evergreens that resent having their roots dry	• Often difficult to support or stake • Only available for about six months of the year (when the plant is dormant) • Larger specimens can be very heavy and awkward to handle due to the volume of compost in the burlap

Protecting climbers & wall shrubs

Many fragrant climbers and wall shrubs are only marginally hardy and actually need a wall or fence for protection and warmth as well as for support. During cold winter periods, however, additional protection may be required to ensure that these plants come through the winter unharmed and produce flowers, fruit and fragrance the following year.

WHAT YOU NEED

Tools: Secateurs; screwdriver; scissors; staple gun
Materials: Garden twine or twist ties; L-brackets or cup hooks; screws; garden fleece; long bamboo canes

In spring, summer and autumn, the residual heat provided by supporting walls or fences can often be sufficient to help fragrant climbers and wall shrubs thrive rather than struggle, making the difference to whether a plant can flower and produce fruit. During the cold winter months, however, climbers such as the passion flower (*Passiflora*), shrubs such as Spanish broom (*Spartium junceum*), and fan-trained trees such as myrtle (*Luma*) and *Ceanothus* may all need additional protection.

A fixed, but adjustable, cover offers the best option, so that it can be raised on warm days and lowered for cold spells. Any insulation material used should allow some light to the plant, and allow some air-flow so that the plant does not suffer from fungal rots.

Should the weather turn warm for a period of time, the protection can be rolled up to allow the sun to warm the plant. This will help to prevent the plant from starting into growth too early in the year. It will also prevent the existing growth from becoming too soft and will discourage any harmful pests and diseases from harbouring under the shelter.

> **Tip:** Growing some of the more tender climbers, such as passion flowers (*Passiflora*), through evergreen shrubs will also provide them with some winter protection.

Trim the plant to remove any damaged growth and tie in any loose or rubbing shoots. Fix four brackets or hooks into the fence or wall – two just above the climber and two near the base of the plant. Both pairs should be about 1.8m (6ft) apart.

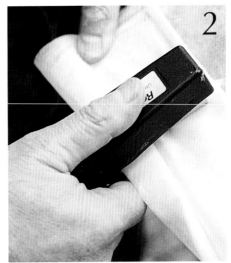

Cut a length of garden fleece 1.8m (6ft) wide and long enough to cover the full height of the plant; allow an extra 10cm (4in) at the top and the bottom. Fold over these 10cm (4in) ends and staple them in position.

Thread a 2m (7ft) cane through the fold at the top the fleece.

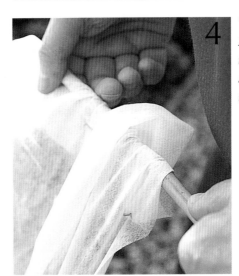

Thread another 2m (7ft) cane through the fold at the bottom of the fleece.

Hang one cane between the top pair of brackets, or over the top hooks, and fix in place.

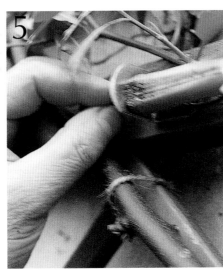

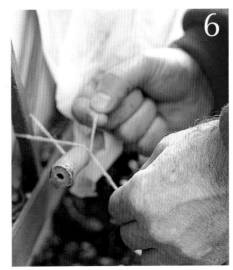

Allow the fleece to drape down in front of the plant before fixing the bottom cane into the lower pair of brackets, or under the bottom hooks.

TREES

Amomyrtus luma
H 7m (23ft) S 4m (13ft)
Sun
Well-drained
Any Z9

This multi-stemmed evergreen tree has an upright habit and beautiful smooth bark that becomes loose and scaly with age. The lance-shaped aromatic leaves are a coppery bronze colour when young, changing to a glossy dark green with age. They are about 2–3cm (1in) long and arranged in opposite pairs along orange-brown stems. From late winter onwards, sweetly scented creamy white flowers are borne in clusters of up to 10 on the branches. The flowers are often followed by aromatic, edible, reddish-black fruits later in the year. Propagate by sowing seed in a cold frame during spring or taking semi-ripe cuttings in late summer.

Azara microphylla
H 10m (32ft) S 4m (13ft)
Sun
Well-drained/moderate
Any Z7

Originating from Chile and Argentina, this is an evergreen tree or large shrub with slender arching branches and oval-shaped, glossy dark green leaves with a finely toothed margin, often paler on the underside. In late winter and into spring, dense clusters of greenish-yellow, vanilla-scented flowers up to 1cm (½in) across are produced. Prune immediately after flowering by cutting the flower-bearing shoots back to 4–5 buds. This is the hardiest azara and is a perfect choice for growing against a hot sunny wall or as a tree in a sheltered garden. Propagate by taking semi-ripe cuttings from the new side shoots in mid- to late summer.

Cornus mas
H 5m (16ft) S 5m (16ft)
Sun
Well-drained
Any Z5

The cornelian cherry is a small
hardy tree that produces fragrant
yellow blossoms in the depths of
winter and well into spring. The
small flowers form tight, golden
yellow clusters held close to the
naked, twiggy branches. By mid-
spring, glossy, broadly oval-shaped,
mid-green leaves are produced in
opposite pairs along the branches
after the flowers have faded. There
are several different cultivars of
this plant that are less vigorous
and provide additional interest
at other times of the year, such
as *C. m.* 'Aurea', and *C. m.*
'Variegata'. Propagate by sowing
seed outdoors in autumn.

Eucalyptus perriniana
H 10m (32ft) S 5m (16ft)
Sun
Well-drained
Acid/neutral Z8

Eucalyptus are interesting evergreen
trees grown mainly for their
aromatic blue-grey, leathery leaves
and peeling stems. The leaf shape
varies with the age of the plant –
the juvenile leaves are almost
circular but, as the plant matures,
the new leaves are strap-like and
a blue-green colour. In the early
years, the stem is blue-grey but,
as the tree ages, the old outer
bark peels away and hangs in
long strips before falling off. Some
species, such as *E. pulverulenta*,
produce clusters of up to three
white flowers in winter. Propagate
by sowing seed in spring.

Prunus mume
H 9m (29ft) S 9m (29ft)
Sun
Well-drained
Any Z6

This deciduous tree is known as
the Japanese apricot, although it
originates from China and Korea.
It has a spreading habit and the
rounded tapered leaves are up
to 10cm (4in) long, dark green in
colour and held on arching green
shoots. In late winter and early
spring, before the leaves emerge,
sweetly fragrant, cup-shaped
flowers up to 2.5cm (1in) across
are carried in pairs along the
branches. Flower colour varies
from pure white through to dark
pink. Later, rounded, yellow,
hairy, apricot-like edible fruits
are produced. Propagate by taking
softwood cuttings in summer or
sowing seed in autumn.

SHRUBS

Coronilla valentina subsp. **glauca**
H 1m (3ft) S 1m (3ft)
Sun
Well-drained
Any Z9

This shrub originates from south-eastern Europe and has a dense, bushy habit with slender, twiggy growth and bluish-green leaves up to 5cm (2in) long. These evergreen leaves are divided into segments, often as many as nine in total. Clusters of up to 14 bright yellow, sweetly scented, pea-like flowers are produced in late winter and early spring and again in late summer, and often followed by slender pods up to 5cm (2in) long. There are a number of forms of this plant, including *C. v.* subsp. *glauca* 'Citrina' (pale yellow flowers) and *C. v.* subsp. *glauca* 'Variegata' (creamy white margin to the leaves). Propagate by sowing seed in a cold frame as soon as it is ripe or taking semi-ripe cuttings in late summer.

Daphne sericea
H 50cm (20in) S 50cm (20in)
Sun
Moderate
Acid/neutral Z8

This slow-growing evergreen shrub benefits from some shelter from cold winds and grows with a compact, rounded habit and glossy dark green leaves with a downy underside. It produces a spectacular display of intensely fragrant, clove-scented flowers in late winter and early spring. These are pinkish-purple with white markings, carried in clusters of up to 15 blooms. On a warm, calm day, the scent carries for a great distance around the plant. Prune only to remove dead or damaged wood and move as little as possible because it resents disturbance. Propagate by taking semi-ripe cuttings in summer.

Erica x darleyensis
H 30cm (12in) S 60cm (2ft)
Sun
Well-drained/moderate
Acid Z6

A hybrid between *E. carnea* and *E. erigena*, the Darley Dale heath forms a dense, bushy evergreen shrub with small, narrow, lance-shaped leaves that are slightly grooved and mid-green in colour. White to rose-pink urn-shaped flowers up to 6mm (¼in) long are carried in spikes up to 10cm (4in) long from late winter and into early spring. The cultivar *E.* x *darleyensis* 'Furzey' produces masses of honey-scented flowers. This plant must have an acid soil. Propagate by taking semi-ripe cuttings from the new shoots in mid- to late summer and placing them in a cold frame, or by mound layering in spring.

Erica x veitchii
H 2m (7ft) S 75cm (30in)
Sun
Well-drained/moderate
Neutral Z8

Veitch's heath is a hybrid between
E. arborea and *E. lusitanica*. It forms
an erect, open shrub with small,
narrow, mid-green evergreen leaves.
From late winter into spring, it
produces 6mm (¼in) long white,
urn-shaped flowers in spikes up to
30cm (12in) long. The cultivar *E.* x
veitchii 'Exeter' produces a strong
display of scented flowers. This plant
is unusual among heathers in that it
will tolerate some lime in the soil,
although it prefers an acid soil.
Propagate by taking semi-ripe
cuttings from the new shoots in
mid- to late summer and placing
them in a cold frame.

Eupatorium sordidum
H 3m (10ft) S 2.5m (8ft)
Sun/partial shade
Moist
Alkaline Z10

A native of Mexico, this is a large,
bushy, rounded, deciduous shrub,
with young stems that have a
covering of reddish woolly hairs.
The deep-green leaves are arranged
in opposite pairs and are broadly
spear-shaped and approximately
10cm (4in) long. They have a finely
toothed margin, pointed tip and a
red felt-like coating on the lower
surface. From late autumn into
winter, the tips of the tall stems bear
violet flowers in broad, rounded
clusters up to 12cm (5in) across,
with a strong resinous fragrance.
Propagate by sowing seed or taking
softwood tip cuttings in spring.

Hamamelis x intermedia
H 3m (10ft) S 4m (13ft)
Sun/partial shade
Moderate
Acid/neutral Z5

The witch hazels are very distinctive
and beautiful deciduous shrubs that
produce attractive winter flower
displays on the bare branches.
The sweetly fragrant flowers have
a twisted, spidery appearance, with
small, feathery, slightly curled petals
that are mainly coloured in various
shades of yellow, although some
cultivars have darker flowers in
shades of coppery red. The large
leaves are mid-green in colour,
broadly oval and provide a stunning
display in autumn when they turn
shades of yellow, orange, scarlet
and red before falling from the
branches. Propagate by taking
softwood cuttings in late summer
or by grafting onto a rootstock
in mid-winter.

SHRUBS

Lonicera x _purpusii_
H 2m (7ft) S 2.5m (8ft)
Sun/shade
Moderate
Any Z6

This winter-flowering shrubby
honeysuckle is grown for its fragrant
flowers, which are arranged in pairs
and are usually carried on the bare
branches in small clusters. The
flowers are basically tubular in
shape, opening out to a broad
mouth, and are usually white in
colour with pale yellow to golden
markings. The deciduous to semi-
evergreen leaves are broadly oval in
shape, and mid- to deep green in
colour. They are carried in pairs on
thin, twiggy, reddish-purple stems,
gradually developing an open,
spreading habit. Propagate by taking
hardwood cuttings of non-flowering
shoots in winter or softwood
cuttings in mid-summer.

Mahonia lomariifolia
H 3m (10ft) S 2m (7ft)
Partial shade
Well-drained
Any Z7

Originating from western China,
this tough, hardy shrub has an
upright habit and glossy, dark green,
leathery evergreen leaves up to
60cm (2ft) long and sub-divided to
make up a compound leaf of many
lance-shaped, sharply toothed
leaflets. From late autumn until
mid-winter, it produces flowers with
a strong, distinctive fragrance. They
are a rich yellow and carried on the
shoot tips in dense upright spikes up
to 20cm (8in) long. The flowers are
often followed by black oval-shaped
berries in summer. Propagate by
taking semi-ripe cuttings in late
summer or early autumn and
placing them in a cold frame.

Mahonia x _media_
H 4m (13ft) S 3m (10ft)
Partial shade
Well-drained
Any Z7

A hybrid of _M. japonica_ and _M.
lomarifolia_, this hardy shrub has an
upright habit and glossy evergreen
leaves composed of many lance-
shaped leaflets. From late autumn
until early spring, it produces dense
spikes of yellow flowers, up to
40cm (16in) long, that have a strong
lily-of-the-valley fragrance. A
cultivar worth considering for a
smaller garden is _M._ x _m._ 'Winter
Sun', which has arching spikes of
bright yellow flowers. Propagate by
taking semi-ripe cuttings in late
summer or early autumn and
placing them in a cold frame.

Sarcococca hookeriana
H 1.5m (5ft) S 2m (7ft)
Shade
Moderate
Any Z6

This hardy evergreen shrub, commonly known as the Christmas box, has a suckering habit and often forms a dense thicket of growth. The tough, leathery leaves are broadly lance-shaped and a mid- to dark green colour, carried on sturdy, erect green stems. In winter, clusters of white, sweetly fragrant flowers are produced in the leaf joints, to be followed by purple-black fruits later in the year. *Sarcococca hookeriana* var. *digyna*, has narrower leaves. Propagate by sowing seed in a cold frame as soon as it is ripe, by taking semi-ripe cuttings in late summer or by removing suckers from the plants soon after flowering.

Skimmia japonica
H 3m (10ft) S 5m (16ft)
Sun
Moderate
Any Z7

The skimmias are slow-growing, hardy evergreens, with thick, leathery, broadly oval-shaped leaves that are aromatic when crushed and carried on stocky, reddish-green stems. The male and female flowers are often reddish-pink in bud before developing as spikes of white, sweetly scented blooms on separate plants from late winter well into spring. These are followed by orange-red berries on the female plants, which persist throughout the following autumn and winter. Skimmias are ideal for inner city gardening because they are tolerant of atmospheric pollution. Propagate by taking semi-ripe cuttings in late summer and placing them in a cold frame.

Viburnum x bodnantense 'Dawn'
H 2m (7ft) S 1.5m (5ft)
Sun/partial shade
Moderate
Any Z7

A spectacular upright shrub for winter colour, this plant will produce its clusters of rich pink flowers on bare stems continuously from late autumn until early spring, although it will pause in periods of severe weather. On a warm, calm day, the sweet fragrance will carry some distance from the plant. As the flowers fade, the coarse-looking leaves begin to emerge, bronze-green at first, ageing to dark green. It is ideal for the back of a border but should be accessible so that the fragrance can be appreciated. Prune only to maintain the health of the plant. Propagate by taking soft-tip cuttings in summer.

CLIMBERS & WALL SHRUBS

Abeliophyllum distichum
H 1.5m (5ft) S 1.5m (5ft)
Sun
Well-drained
Any Z5

A native of Korea, this attractive shrub has an open, spreading habit and makes an excellent wall shrub with thin, light brown, arching shoots. This plant can reach over 2.5m (8ft) when grown against a wall. The oval-shaped deciduous leaves are arranged in opposite pair. They are about 8cm (3in) long and a dull matt green colour, often turning a reddish-purple in autumn. In late winter and early spring, small, sweetly fragrant, cross-shaped white flowers with pink markings are produced in long slender clusters in the leaf joints. Propagate by layering or taking semi-ripe cuttings in summer.

Chimonanthus praecox
H 4m (13ft) S 3m (10ft)
Sun
Well-drained
Any Z7

The wintersweet is a large shrub ideal for training against a wall or fence. It has tough, waxy flowers that have narrow petals, coloured pale translucent yellow with a purple centre, opening from mid-winter onwards. The blooms have a delicate spicy fragrance. Although hardy, this large, upright shrub is slow to establish and may take several years before flowers are produced. The lance-shaped, glossy mid-green, deciduous leaves are up to 20cm (8in) long and produced after flowering has finished. Propagate by sowing seed in a cold frame as soon as it is ripe or taking softwood cuttings in summer.

Edgeworthia chrysantha
H 1.5m (5ft) S 1.5m (5ft)
Sun/partial shade
Moderate
Any Z8

Commonly known as the paper bush, this deciduous shrub has an open habit and lax branches, gradually forming a dome-shaped bush. The oval-shaped dark green leaves are up to 15cm (6in) long and usually clustered close to the branch tips. In late winter and early spring, dense clusters of small, yellow, tubular flowers around 5cm (2in) across are produced, each flower with a strong fragrance of cloves. This plant may need protection and for this reason is better trained against a wall. Propagate by sowing seed in containers in a cold frame in autumn or by taking semi-ripe cuttings in summer.

Jasminum nudiflorum
H 3m (10ft) S 3m (10ft)
Sun
Moderate
Any Z6

Commonly known as the winter jasmine, this popular deciduous plant is outstanding in winter, especially when grown as a wall shrub. The thin, whippy, almost leafless stems are square in shape and green in colour, which gives the whole plant an evergreen appearance. It is much valued for its small, sweetly fragrant, tubular, star-shaped yellow flowers, which open from late autumn through until early spring. The variegated form of this plant, J. n. 'Aureum', has golden yellow splashes on the leaves. This plant can be grown in almost any situation and almost any soil. Propagate in autumn by taking semi-ripe cuttings or tip layers, which occur naturally wherever the stems touch the soil.

Lonicera fragrantissima
H 2m (7ft) S 3m (10ft)
Sun/shade
Moderate
Any Z5

This is a very attractive deciduous shrub and produces one of the most fragrant winter displays on the naked branches. The plant produces frequent flushes of honey-scented, creamy white flowers from late autumn to early spring. The deciduous to semi-evergreen leaves are broadly oval-shaped and carried in pairs on thin, twiggy stems with attractive light brown bark. The leaves are deep green on the upper surface and bluish-green beneath. This shrub is often grown against a wall to keep its spreading habit and arching branches under control. Propagate by taking hardwood cuttings of non-flowering shoots in winter or softwood cuttings in mid-summer.

Viburnum tinus
H 3m (10ft) S 3m (10ft)
Sun/partial shade
Moderate
Any Z7

This hardy evergreen shrub is commonly called the laurustinus. It has upright growth when young but develops a rather open, round-topped and spreading habit as it ages. The smooth, broadly oval, dark green leaves have paler green undersides and are arranged in pairs along the dark greenish-brown stems, with each stem ending in a flat cluster of small, lightly clove-scented, tubular white flowers, which last throughout the winter months. Possibly the best plant is V. t. 'Eve Price', which has flowers of a deep rose-pink in bud, opening to white flushed with pink. Propagate by taking semi-ripe cuttings in early summer.

HERBACEOUS PLANTS & BULBS

Crocus chrysanthus Group
H 5cm (2in) S 2.5cm (1in)
Sun/partial shade
Well-drained
Any Z4

This large group of hardy crocus hybrids related to *C. chrysanthus* flower in late winter and early spring. They have short, dull grey to mid-green leaves and each plant can produce up to four sweetly scented flowers. There is a vast range of flower colours, ranging from white and cream through to pale and golden yellow, orange and deeper shades such as blues, mauves and purples. This group of plants is suitable for forcing indoors and, after flowering, they can be planted out to naturalise in the garden. Propagate by dividing when the plant is dormant after the leaves have died down.

Cyclamen coum
H 7.5cm (3in) S 10cm (4in)
Shade
Well-drained
Any Z6

This hardy cyclamen is an incredibly tough little tuberous perennial plant, with almost round or broadly oval-shaped dark green leaves with pronounced silver or grey markings held above the ground on curling red stems. *C. coum* produces delicately scented flowers varying from pure white to shades of pink through to carmine red in the depths of winter, often all growing tightly grouped together in the same group or colony. There is a form with white flowers and dark purple-red markings named *C. coum* f. *albissimum.* Propagate by sowing seed as soon as it is ripe.

Cymbidium
H 60cm (2ft) S 1m (3ft)
Partial shade
Well-drained
Any Z9

Originating from tropical south-east Asia and Australia, these versatile plants have become popular houseplants in recent years. The best cymbidium orchids for use in the home are the modern cultivars with small pseudobulbs. They have long, arching, strap-like leaves up to 40cm (16in) long, usually mid- to light green in colour, with long slender stems bearing as many as 30 flowers up to 8cm (3in) across in a single season. The blooms can vary in colour from blackish-red through shades of pink, yellow, white and even green, and are often fragrant. Propagate by dividing after flowering.

HERBACEOUS PLANTS & BULBS

Eranthis
H 7.5cm (3in) S 5cm (2in)
Sun/shade
Well-drained
Any Z5

The winter aconite (*E. hyemalis*) is much valued for its early flowering. In late winter and early spring, small, yellow, buttercup-like flowers appear, with a green frill of leaves, held above the ground on a green stem. The flowers have a light, sweet fragrance. *E.* x *tubergenii* is a slightly earlier flowering hybrid of *E. cilicica* and *E. hyemalis*, and *E.* x *t.* 'Guinea Gold' produces deeper golden yellow flowers with a deliciously sweet fragrance. Treated as a bulb, it is actually a tuberous hardy perennial, with attractive pale green, deeply cut leaves. Propagate by dividing when the plant is dormant after the leaves have died down.

Galanthus nivalis
H 10cm (4in) S 10cm (4in)
Partial shade
Well-drained
Any Z4

The snowdrop is a very hardy winter-flowering bulb that has a clump-forming habit. It is grown for its pretty, white, honey-scented blooms. The pendulous flowers are produced from mid-winter onwards, carried singly on slender green stalks. The flat, strap-shaped leaves are a dull mid-green with a slightly bluish sheen to them, arranged in pairs usually one either side of the flower stalk. Several cultivars have started to become popular. *G. n.* 'Flore-pleno' has double white flowers and *G. n.* 'Samuel Arnott' produces larger flowers up to 4cm (1½in) in length. Propagate by lifting and dividing clumps immediately after flowering has finished.

Narcissus papyraceus
H 40cm (16in) S 5–15cm (2–6in)
Sun
Moderate
Any Z8

This plant is often called the paper-white narcissus, and is even sold as *N.* 'Paper White'. It has long, broad, mid-green leaves, held very erect above ground level, and in the centre of each group of leaves is a round, mid-green flower stem that carries up to 10 clear white flowers that are very fragrant. Although this is a winter-flowering plant, it is not as hardy as some species and will benefit from shelter, so ensure that a small amount of frost protection is provided. Lift and divide every 3–5 years, 6 weeks after flowering.

GLOSSARY & INDEX GLOSSARY & INDEX...
GLOSSARY
GLOSSARY & INDEX GLOSSARY & INDEX

GLOSSARY

Acclimatisation (acclimation)
Adjusting plants to different conditions (usually cooler) than those in which they are growing

Aerate (soil)
Loosen by physical or mechanical means to allow the penetration of air; for example, using a tined fork to aerate the lawn

Alkaline
A substance (soil) with a pH value of 7 or higher

Alpine
A plant that originates from mountainous regions; often applied to rock garden plants

Alternate (buds/leaves)
Leaves that occur at different levels on opposite sides of the stem

Aminoides
A chemical found in some white or off-white flowers that makes them smell of ammonia

Annual
A plant that completes its reproduction cycle in one year

Anther
The pollen-bearing tip of the flower's stamen (male floral parts)

Apex
The tip of a shoot or branch

Apical bud
The uppermost bud in the growing point of a stem (also known as the *terminal bud*)

Aquatic
Any plant that grows in water (may be anchored or free floating)

Aromatic
Spicy fragrance usually emitted from leaves

Axil
The angle at the point where the leaf or branch joins the main stem of a plant

Axillary bud
A bud that occurs in the leaf axil

Backfill
The operation of refilling a trench or hole in the ground

Bare-root
Plants that are offered for sale with no soil on their roots (usually grown in a field and dug up for sale)

Bark
A protective layer of cells that occurs on the outer surface of the plant's roots and stems of woody plants

Basal
A shoot or bud arising from the base of a plant

Basal plate
The compressed stem of a bulb

Base dressing
Fertiliser or organic matter incorporated into the soil before planting or sowing

Bedding plants
Plants arranged in mass groupings (beds) to form a colourful temporary display

Biennial
A plant that completes its growing cycle in two growing seasons — germinates and produces roots and leaves in its first year, flowers and produces seed before dying in the second year; for example, foxglove

Blanch
a) To exclude light from sections of a plant in order to keep the tissues soft and supple
b) To plunge sections of a plant in hot water in order to keep the tissues soft and supple

Bleeding
The excessive flow of sap from spring-pruned plants

Blind bud
A bud that fails to produce a terminal bud

Bog plant
A plant that prefers to grow in damp soil (also known as a *marginal*)

Bract
A modified leaf often brightly coloured to appear flower-like; for example, clematis

Branch
A shoot growing directly from the main stem of a woody plant

Break
A shoot growing from a bud as a result of pruning

Broadcasting
The technique of spreading fertiliser or seeds randomly

Bud
A condensed shoot containing an embryonic shoot or flower

Bud union
The point where a cultivar is budded onto a rootstock

Budding
A propagation technique joining two (or more) plants together

Bulb
A storage organ consisting of thick fleshy leaves arranged on a compressed stem (see *basal plate*) found below soil level

Bush
A multi-branched plant with a number of branches of similar size

Calcicole
A plant that prefers a soil that is alkaline (pH 7+), usually a limey soil

Calcifuge
A plant that prefers a soil that is acidic (pH 7–), usually a peaty or organic soil

Callus
The plant tissue that forms as a protective cover over a cut or wounded surface

Calyx
The outer green ring or whorl of a flower, made up of a number of sepals enclosing the petals

Capillary watering
Where plants draw up water into a container from a saturated base

Chilling
A period of low temperature (usually 2°C/36°F) required by plants during dormancy to stimulate flower development

Chipping
Cutting bulbs into small sections to propagate them

Chlorophyll
The green plant pigment that is mainly responsible for light absorption and photosynthesis in plants

Climber
A self-supporting plant capable of growing vertically

Cloche
A small, clear, portable structure used for protecting plants

Clone
A collective term for a number of plants that have been propagated from a single individual

Cold frame
A low, clear, portable or permanent structure used for protecting plants from the elements

Companion planting
Growing certain plant combinations close together to overcome pest and disease problems organically

Compound leaf
A leaf consisting of a number of small segments (leaflets)

Compost
a) Potting media made to a standard formula; loam- or peat-based
b) Well-rotted organic matter such as garden waste

Conifer
A classification of plants that have naked ovules often borne in cones, and narrow needle-like foliage

Corm
An underground modified stem forming a storage organ

Cotyledon
The seed leaves (first leaves) on a seedling; can be:
a) Dicotyledon – plants with two seed leaves
b) Monocotyledon – plants with one seed leaf

Crown
The growing point of a herbaceous perennial originating at soil level

Cultivar
A plant form that originated in cultivation rather than having been found growing in the wild

Cutting
A portion of a plant that is used for propagation

Dead-heading
The deliberate removal of dead flower heads or seed-bearing fruits

Deciduous
Plants that produce new leaves in the spring and shed them in the autumn

Dieback
The death of plant growth downwards from the shoot tip

Disbudding
The removal of unwanted buds to produce fewer, but much larger, flowers

Distillation
The process of heating liquids to get the different components to separate, usually as vapour

Division
A method of propagation that is used to increase the number of plants by splitting them up into smaller units

Dormancy
A period of reduced growth through the winter

Drainage
The free movement of surplus water through the soil/compost

Drill
A narrow straight line used for sowing seeds into

Dry storage
A method of storing edible plants in readiness for use

Earthing up
Mounding up the soil around the base of a plant

Edging shears
Long-handled shears used for trimming lawn edges from a standing position

Enfleurage
The extraction of perfumes from flowers using fats

Epicormic shoots
Shoots that develop from dormant adventitious buds on the main stem of a plant (often referred to as 'water shoots')

Ericaceous
A member of the *Erica* family, which likes acid soil conditions (see *calcifuge*)

Essential oil
A volatile oil that gives plants their characteristic smell and that is usually produced and stored in the petals or sepals of flowers, but is also found in leaves, bark and roots

Evergreen
Plants that retain their actively growing leaves through the winter

Fertile
A soil rich in nutrients and biological life

Fertiliser
An organic or inorganic compound used to supply nutrition to plants to help them grow

Fibrous roots
Fine, multi-branched roots of a plant

Flat
A low-sided box or tray used for propagating young plants or seeds

Fleece (horticultural)
Light, woven, geotextile material used to protect plants from frost or as a barrier against insect pests

Floating mulch
A sheet of plastic or woven material used for protecting plants from frost, this type of mulch stretches with the plants as they grow

Flower
The part of a plant (often highly coloured) that contains the reproductive organs

Force
To induce plants to start growing earlier than they usually would

Fork
A tined digging implement used for cultivating soil

Formative pruning
A pruning method carried out on young plants to establish a desired plant shape and branch structure

Fragrance
Sweet scent or pleasant smell

Framework
The main permanent branch structure of a woody plant

Frost pocket
A location where cold air accumulates

Fruit
The seed-bearing vessel on a plant

Fruit set
The successful formation of fruits

Fungicide
A chemical used to control fungal disease

Germination
The physical and chemical process by which a seed develops into a plant

Glycoside
A derivative formed from a simple sugar and another molecule by the elimination of water

Graft union
The point where a cultivar is grafted onto a rootstock

Grafting
A propagation method involving the artificial joining of two or more separate plants together

Greenhouse
A glass- or plastic-clad structure used to grow plants under controlled (protected) conditions

Ground cover
The term used to describe low-growing plants

Gum
Any viscous matter exuded by a plant that hardens on contact with the air

Half hardy
A plant that can tolerate low temperatures but is killed by frost

Hardening-off
Adjusting plants to different conditions (usually cooler) than those in which they are growing

Hardy
A plant that can tolerate temperatures below freezing without protection

Harvesting
The gathering or collecting of plant produce for storage or consumption

GLOSSARY

Herbaceous
A non-woody plant with an annual top and a perennial root system or storage organ

Herbicide
A chemical used to kill weeds

Hoeing
A method of shallow cultivation used to kill weed seedlings

Houseplants
Tender plants grown indoors for decoration

Humus
The organic residue of decayed organic material

Hybrid
A plant derived from crossing two other genetically different plants

Indole
A natural plant chemical responsible for the rotten smell of some plants (for example, *Rosa foetida*) and the cloying sweet scent of others (lilies and jonquils)

Inorganic
A man-made chemical compound (one that does not contain carbon). Inorganic fertiliser is produced artificially or refined from naturally occurring chemicals

Insecticide
A chemical used to kill insects

Irrigation
A general term used for the application of water

Lateral
A sideshoot arising from an axillary bud

Layering
A propagation technique whereby roots are formed on a stem before it is detached from the parent plant

Leaching
The loss of nutrients by washing them through the soil

Leader
The main dominant shoot or stem of the plant (usually the terminal shoot)

Leaf
The main lateral organ of a green plant

Leaf mould
A compost-like substance formed from partially decomposed leaves

Leaflet
One of the small segments of a compound leaf

Lime
An alkaline substance formed from calcium

Loam
A soil comprising equal proportions of clay, sand and silt

Loppers
Long-handled, secateur-like pruners used for pruning thick branches

Marginal plant
A plant that prefers to grow in damp soil conditions or partially submerged in water

Medium
(see *compost*)

Monoecious
Plants that carry both male and female flowers on the same plant

Mowing
Cutting down lawn grass to a required height

Mulch
A layer of material applied to cover the soil

Multi-row system
A method of growing plants close together to regulate their overall size (also to control weeds)

Mutation
A plant change or variation occurring by chance, often referred to as a 'sport'

Naturalise
To establish bulbs or other plants in grass so that they appear to have occurred there naturally

Nutrients
The minerals (fertilisers) used to feed plants

Olfactory
Related to the sense of smell

Organic
Materials derived from decomposed animal or plant remains

Outdoor storage
A method of storing produce outside but with some protection; for example, a potato clamp

Oxygenator
An aquatic plant which releases oxygen into the water

Pan
a) A shallow terracotta dish used for growing plants
b) A compacted layer of soil that impedes drainage and root penetration into the soil

Peat
Decayed sphagnum mosses, or rushes and sedges

Perennial
Strictly any plant that has a life cycle of more than three years

Pesticide
The generic name for chemicals used to control pests and diseases

pH
A measure of acidity and alkalinity in a soil

Photosynthesis
The production of the compounds needed for plant growth by the synthesis of chlorophyll, light energy, carbon dioxide and water

Pinching out
The removal (usually with finger and thumb) of the growing point of a shoot to encourage the development of lateral shoots

Plunging
A method of inserting plants into their growing site without removing the pot from around their root ball

Potting on
Transferring a plant to a larger container

Potting up
Transferring young plants or seedlings from the seed bed/tray to a larger container

Propagation
Techniques used to multiply the number of plants

Propagator
a) A structure used to propagate plants in
b) A person who propagates plants

Protoplasm
A complex substance regarded as the physical basis of life (it can spontaneously move and reproduce), which forms the living matter of all plant cells and tissues

Pruning
The practice of cutting plants to improve their growth or train them to grow in a certain way

Raised bed system
A system of growing plants in beds of soil above the surrounding soil level

Rambler
A vigorous trailing plant with a scrambling habit

Rhizome
A specialised underground stem that lies horizontally in the soil

Root
The underground support system of a plant

Root ball
The combined root system and surrounding soil/compost of a plant

Root-balled
Plants that have been dug up with the roots enclosed in a block of soil, which is held in place with hessian sacking or a similar material

Root pruning
The cutting of live plant roots to control the vigour of a plant

Rooting
The production of roots, usually from cuttings

Rootstock
The root system onto which a cultivar is budded or grafted

Runner
A stem that grows horizontally close to the ground, such as strawberry

Sap
The juice or 'blood' of a plant

Scale
A modified leaf of a bulb used for propagation

Scarification
A method of damaging the seed coat to encourage germination

Scion
The propagation material taken from a *cultivar* or variety to be used for budding or grafting

Seed
A cellular structure produced by flowering plants that contains a dormant embryo capable of developing into an adult plant

Seedhead
Any fruit that contains ripe seeds

Shoot
A branch, stem or twig

Shrub
A woody-stemmed plant

Side shoot
A stem arising from a branch, stem or twig

Spur
A short fruit- or flower-bearing branch

Stem
The main shoot of a tree

Stopping
Cutting out the growing point of a shoot to encourage the development of lateral shoots

Storage
A method of keeping plants in an environment that delays ripening and decay

Stratification
The storage of seed in cold/warm conditions to overcome dormancy

Sub-lateral
A side shoot arising from an axillary bud of a lateral shoot

Sub-soil
The layers of soil beneath the topsoil

Sucker
A shoot arising from below ground level

Tannin
An astringent vegetable compound

Tap root
The large main root of a plant

Tender
A plant which is killed or damaged by low temperatures (–10°C/50°F) and frost damage

Tendril
A thin, twining, stem-like structure used by some climbing plants to support themselves

Terminal bud
The uppermost bud in the growing point of a stem (also known as the *apical bud*)

Thatch
A layer of dead organic matter on the soil surface in a lawn

Thinning
The removal of branches to improve the quality of those remaining

Tip prune
Cutting back the growing point of a shoot to encourage the development of lateral shoots

Top-dressing
An application of fertiliser or bulky organic matter added to the soil surface and often incorporated around the base of the plant

Topiary
The practice of trimming plants into formal shapes and patterns

Training
The practice of making plants grow into a particular shape or pattern

Transplanting
Moving plants from one growing area to another in order to provide them with more growing room

Tree
A woody perennial plant usually consisting of a clear stem or trunk, and a framework or head of branches

Trunk
The main stem of a mature tree

Tuber
A root or stem modified to form a storage organ

Tying down
A method of using string ties for training shoots into a horizontal position

Union (graft union)
The point where a cultivar is grafted onto a rootstock

Variegated
Plant parts (usually leaves) marked with a blotched irregular pattern of colours such as gold or silver on a base colour of green

Vegetative growth
Non-flowering stem growth

Virus
A debilitating organism which lives inside the plant (there is no cure)

Volatile oil
An oil that evaporates easily. Highly volatile plant oils (lavender) evaporate more quickly and provide a milder scent than plant oils with low volatility (patchouli, cedar), which evaporate more slowly

Waterlogging
A condition in soil where all of the air spaces are filled (saturated) with water and oxygen is excluded

Whorl
The arrangement of three or more leaves, buds or shoots arising from the same level

Wilt
The partial collapse of a plant due to water loss or root damage

Wind-rock
The loosening of a plants roots caused by wind

INDEX

ACKNOWLEDGEMENTS

The authors would like to thank Janis Wales, Alice, Alistair, Con, Gary and Mark from the 'Gardening Which' gardens at Capel Manor College, Middlesex. Julie Ryan and the staff at Capel Manor, particularly, Ian, Carl, Peter and Terry. Craig and the staff at Frensham Garden Centre, Frensham, Surrey. Photographers Andrea Jones and Mark Winwood. Fiona and Linda at Limelight Management. Iain MacGregor, Anna Osborn and Anna Cheifetz from Murdoch Books. Chris and Nick Bradley for being so patient when we were busy.

Andrea Jones would like to thank all the gardeners and garden owners that helped her research and select plants for the photography of this book in the UK, Europe and USA. Special thanks to Peter Gregory for his continual support and assistance.

CREDITS

Photographs courtesy of The Alhambra, Granada, Spain (p.90, 142); David Austin Roses, Wolverhampton (p.42, 84, 117 left, 189 right); Brightstone and District Horticultural Society, Chelsea flower show 2001 (p.38); Andreas Bruun, Køge, Denmark (p.68); Chanticleer Gardens, Philadelphia, PA, USA (p.46); Crûg Farm Plants, Caernarfon, North Wales (p.48, 164, 180 right); Alex Dingwall-Main, Luberon Valley, France (p.49); Peter and Catherine Erskine, Cambo Gardens, Kingsbarns, Fife, Scotland (p.39, 40–41, 45, 74, 155 left, 188 right); Fleur Trouvé (front cover, p. 67 top right, 81, 124, 149); Glamis Castle, Scotland (p.7, 37); Eva and Roland Gustavsson, Sweden (p.67 right, 69 right); Heronswood Nursery, Kingston, WA, USA (p.75 centre); Keukenhof Gardens, Lisse, Holland (p.50, 54); The Marchioness of Salisbury, Hatfield house, Hertfordshire (p.8, 16, 151 right); Mr and Mrs T.K. Marshall, Hunts Court, North Nibley, Gloucestershire (p.189 left); National Trust for Scotland, Crathes Castle, Banchory, Scotland (p.108); Natural Driftwood Sculptures, Bournemouth (p.9, 188 left); Norfolk Lavender Farm, Heacham (p.24); El Novillero, Napa Valley, CA, USA (p.118 centre, 120 centre); Royal Botanic Gardens, Kew (p. 86, 95 and assorted plant portraits); RHS Gardens Wisley, Surrey (p.149 right and assorted plant portraits); St Andrews Botanic Gardens, Fife, Scotland (p.109, 186 right); Westonbirt Arboretum, (p.111 right, 147 centre); Major M.T.N.H. Wills, Miserdon Park Gardens, Stroud, Gloucestershire (p.92, 126, 146 centre).

First published in 2002 by Murdoch Books UK Ltd

ISBN 1 85391 968 3

A catalogue record for this book is available from the British library.

Text copyright © Murdoch Books UK Ltd 2002
All photography copyright © Murdoch Books UK Ltd 2002 except front cover, pages 67 (top right) and 81 (*Murraya paniculata*) and pages 124 and 149 (*Plumeria rubra*) courtesy Fleur Trouvé (www.fleurtrouve.com).

Managing Editor Anna Cheifetz
Project Editor Michelle Pickering
Design Concept & Design Manager Sarah Rock
Plant portraits & garden photography Andrea Jones
Practical photography Mark Winwood

CEO Robert Oerton
Publisher Catie Ziller
Production Manager Lucy Byrne

Colour separation by Colourscan, Singapore
Printed by C&C Offset Printing Co., China

Murdoch Books UK Ltd	UK Distribution	Murdoch Books®
Ferry House	Macmillan Distribution Ltd	Pier 8/9, 23 Hickson Road
51–57 Lacy Road	Houndsmills, Brunell Road	Miller's Point
London SW15 1PR	Basingstoke, Hampshire, RG1 6XS	NSW 2000 Australia
Tel: +44 (0)20 8355 1480	United Kingdom	Tel: +61 (0)2 8220 2000
Fax: +44 (0)20 8355 1499	Tel: +44 (0) 1256 302 707	Fax: +61 (0)2 8220 2558
Murdoch Books UK Ltd is a subsidiary	Fax: +44 (0) 1256 351 437	Murdoch Books® is a trademark
of Murdoch Magazines Pty Ltd	http://www.macmillan-mdl.co.uk	of Murdoch Magazines Pty Ltd